Great Sewing Accesories— to Sew

Great Sewing Accesories— to Sew

Carol Parks

Sterling Publishing Co., Inc.
New York
A Sterling/Lark Book

10 9 8 7 6 5 4 3 2 1

A Sterling/Lark Book

First paperback edition published in 1998 by
  Sterling Publishing Company, Inc.
  387 Park Avenue South, New York, N.Y. 10016

Produced by Altamont Press, Inc.
  50 College Street, Asheville, NC 28801

© 1997 by Altamont Press

Distributed in Canada by Sterling Publishing
% Canadian Manda Group, One Atlantic Avenue, Suite 105
Toronto, Ontario, Canada M6K 3E7

Distributed in Great Britain and Europe by Cassell PLC
Wellington House, 125 Strand, London WC2R 0BB, England

Distributed in Australia by Capricorn Link (Australia) Pty Ltd.
P.O. Box 6651, Baulkham Hills, Business Centre, NSW 2153, Australia

Sterling ISBN 0-8069-9566-1 Trade
          0-8069-9569-6 Paper

Contents

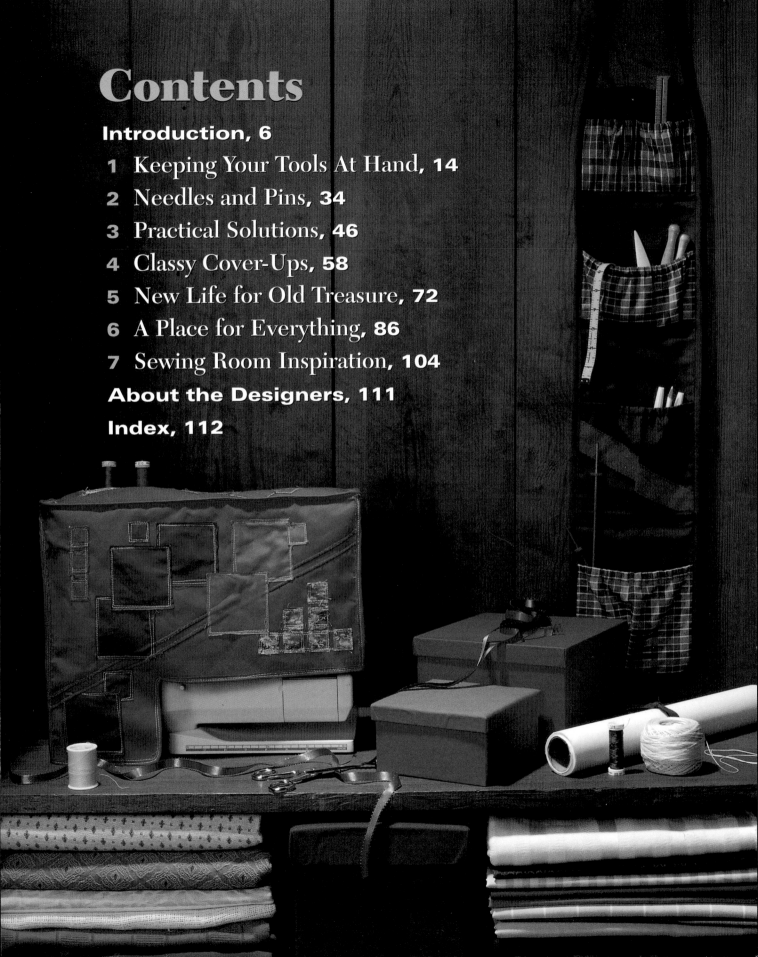

Introduction

THE litany of sewers' wishes seems to be universal: more time to sew, more space, and a solution to the problem of keeping up with an ever-increasing number of tools, gadgets, notions, fabrics, and other essential paraphernalia.

The time problem is the tricky one. You can, of course, quit your job, send the children away to school, volunteer your husband to do charity work during the dinner hour, and have the telephone disconnected. As a less drastic alternative, spend a little time working on the organizational and storage problems. If your precious sewing hours aren't wasted hunting the scissors among stacks of quilting blocks, or digging through boxes to find just the right bit of fusible knit interfacing, you can devote them instead to the pleasurable aspects of sewing.

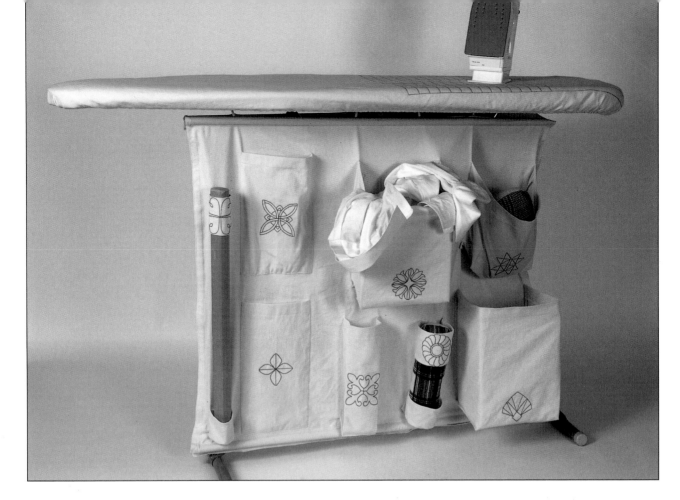

Many of the projects in the following chapters are designed to make the sewing room more efficient. With tools where you can reach them and materials where you can find them, you'll gain hours of sewing time without doing another thing. There are projects, too, that are designed to expedite some of the more time-consuming sewing tasks such as cutting out and pressing.

Take an hour or two to study your sewing space. Look at the equipment you have and the way it is arranged. Are frequently used tools where you can reach them from the sewing chair? Can you find the one you need without searching through cluttered drawers? Are gadgets that are rarely used occupying critical space near the machine?

With an inventory of your tools and equipment in mind, look through the project chapters for ideas to help you organize it all in the way that works best for you. Most of the designs can easily be adapted to fit spaces of all shapes and sizes, and to accommodate any arrangement of tools and notions.

Look for Potential Storage Space

Almost every room has storage space just waiting to be discovered. The narrowest strip of wall can accommodate a floor-to-ceiling pocket organizer that will hold dozens of gadgets and tools. The back of the sewing chair is an ideal spot in which to hang an organizer to keep often-used tools within easy reach. Even the space beneath the ironing board can be put to use.

Look for storage potential under the furniture, up and down the walls, and even at the ceiling itself. Those heavy-duty hooks meant for hanging plants work just as well for holding baskets of scraps or yarn, and can add an interesting decorative element at the same time.

Consider the Aesthetics

Organizing the sewing area provides a great opportunity to decorate it at the same time. While smaller projects offer practical ways to use up fabric scraps, some of the larger ones—such as the wall organizer on page 97—can be as ornamental as they are useful. These can be planned to coordinate with the room's color scheme, or to establish a new one. If one of the large-scale projects is in your plan, buy extra fabric to make a new sewing chair cushion, or perhaps to cover a few storage boxes like those shown at left and on page 101.

The use of a particular technique can serve as a decorative theme too. You might choose a motif to applique on several different pieces, or use fabric paints to add design. Machine embroidery is an ideal way to embellish utilitarian pieces—and offers the chance to try out your machine's fancy stitches and play with some unusual decorative threads.

Gifts for Sewers

Many of the accessories shown on the following pages make thoughtful gifts for friends who sew. While it might not be feasible to make up a hanging organizer that will meet the requirements of someone else's sewing room, a pretty pincushion or needle case is the useful sort of thing we never seem to find time to make for our own use.

About the Projects

Most of the designers who contributed projects for this book are professional sewers. Their ideas have evolved through years of experience and the necessity of making every sewing minute count. They are masters at organization and efficient sewing.

Their designs are meant to work the same way for you: to help you increase your sewing efficiency and to make your sewing time more enjoyable. Most of all, it is hoped that these projects will inspire your own creative schemes and provide you with hours of sewing fun!

How to Hang Things Up

Many of the storage-oriented projects shown throughout the book are made to be hung on a wall to take advantage of otherwise unused space. The instructions for each of these projects include specifics for finishing the piece so that it can be hung or mounted in a particular way; however, your own situation may call for hanging the piece in a different manner and you will want to finish it accordingly. Look at the instructions for similar projects to find alternatives.

Consider the Weight

A good-sized hanging organizer, filled to capacity, can be quite heavy. Allow for the eventual weight of the piece when you determine how to finish it for hanging and how to mount the hardware from which it will hang. Casings or loops incorporated into the piece have to be sturdy enough to bear the weight of the piece, and should be sewn securely. The wall-mounted supports upon which these are hung must be strong enough, and attached securely enough, to support the weight without loosening or pulling out.

Hangers & Hooks

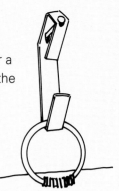

■ A framing shop or good hardware store will offer a variety of decorative hooks that can complement the piece you plan to make. For a piece that is not too heavy, standard nail-in picture hooks can be used behind the piece. These usually have package information as to their load-bearing capacity.

■ Traditional coat hooks, in brass, plastic, or iron, also can be attractive and will support considerable weight. For large or very heavy pieces, attach several of them to a sturdy length of board in the style of a school cloakroom style.

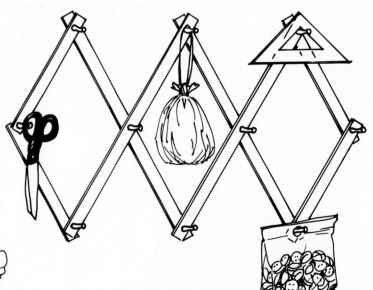

■ A coat rack with hooks attached, or the expanding wooden variety, is a handy device from which to hang all sorts of smaller items.

■ Many older houses and some newer ones feature picture molding at or near the ceiling. Hooks made to fit the molding provide an efficient means of hanging things up and out of the way.

Hanging Security

The safest way to mount hooks for large or very heavy pieces is with screws fastened securely into the studs of the wall. Studs are usually located 16 inches (40.5 cm) apart in a load-bearing wall; 24 inches (61 cm) apart if the wall supports less weight. In older houses, however, suds often seem to be spaced according to some mysterious system of measurement known only to single builder who has long since departed this world.

To locate the studs, try tapping across the wall with a knuckle. At a stud, the sound should be dull and solid; between the studs the sound will be rather hollow. This method works better on drywall than on plaster walls. For best results, invest in a reliable stud-finding device from a hardware store or home center.

To mount the hook, use a number 6 or 8 screw, long enough to extend through the drywall or plaster and well into the stud. If all the hooks needed to hang a piece cannot be located at the studs, try to plan so that at least the center hook or end hooks are in studs. As an alternative, use plastic screw anchors in plaster walls or expansion anchors with drywall.

For very heavy pieces, mount a length of sturdy board across the wall, attaching it to the studs. Attach hooks along the board to hang the piece.

Finishing the Piece for Hanging

The project designers employed a variety of different methods to finish their organizers for hanging. Several of these are described below, and instructions for the individual projects may suggest other options.

■ For a piece that is narrow across the top, sew cord or ribbon (securely!) at each upper corner, then tie or loop it over a decorative hook. If the edges of the piece are bound with bias, like the organizer on page 17, extend the binding to form ties at the top.

■ Sew cafe rings across the upper edge. Cut a dowel or use a curtain rod several inches longer than the width of the piece. Mount hooks to support the ends of the rod. As an alternative, use loops of ribbon or braid to suspend the rod from the hooks.

■ Make a casing across the upper edge and hang the piece as described above.

■ Hem the upper edge of the piece, incorporating a strip of stiff interfacing such as buckram. Attach heavy-duty grommets at intervals along the hem, then hang the piece from a row of decorative hooks.

■ The hanging organizer shown on page 97 is finished this way to support the considerable weight of the piece. Choose sturdy hooks that mount nearly flush with the wall. Cut a length of wooden lattice strip just slightly shorter than the planned finished width of the piece. Near each end, drill a hole large enough to fit over the hook that will be used for hanging. On the backing of the organizer, add a casing below the upper edge that is wide enough to accommodate the lattice strip. Finish the casing approximately 2 to 3 inches (5 to 7.5 cm) inside each edge of the piece.

Bias Bindings

Many of the projects in the following chapters call for bias binding around the edges or across the seams. Bindings of self fabric, or with fabric of a contrasting pattern or color, are much more elegant than commercial bias tape binding that doesn't quite match. Custom bias binding is easy and quick to make if you use the right tools.

To measure and cut the strips, use a rotary cutter with a see-through ruler. Chalk mark the first line on the fabric bias, then measure and cut the strips you need without marking them. With the rotary cutter it is easy to cut perfectly even strips.

If you don't already own them, invest in bias tape makers in several sizes. These gadgets are worth their weight in diamonds for the time they save in pressing under bias-cut edges, and for the excellent results they produce. They are available in a range of sizes to produce double fold tape from approximately ¼ inch (.5 cm) to ¾ inch (2 cm) wide. When a bias fabric strip is pulled through the tape maker, the tool folds in the outer edges so you can press them in place as you pull. Then it's a simple matter to press the center crease if you need double fold tape. Tape makers can be purchased in fabric stores and from mail order notions suppliers.

For the smoothest finished bindings, cut fabric strips on the true fabric bias—at a 45-degree angle to the selvages. Cut the strips to the width needed for the tape maker you are using, or cut them four times the desired finished binding width.

To join bias strips, stitch the ends with right sides together along the straight grain of the fabric as shown. Press the seam open.

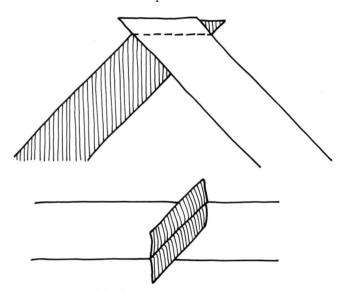

To press a double fold strip without using a tape maker, the fabric in half lengthwise and press. Fold the edge in to the center crease; press.

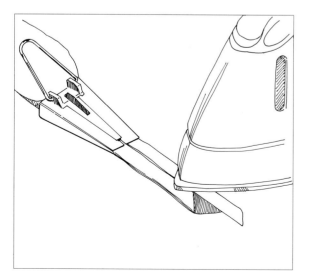

Continuous Bias

When you need considerable yardage, it is easier to join the fabric ends first. You can then cut a continuous strip many yards in length.

1 ▪ Fold a rectangular piece of fabric along the true bias, beginning at a lower corner. Cut along the foldline.

2 ▪ Sew the small triangle to the other edge of the fabric, matching the lengthwise grainlines. Press the seam open.

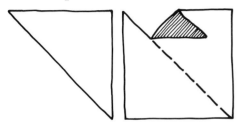

3 ▪ Beginning at one bias-cut end, mark off the bias strip widths.

4 ▪ With right sides together, pin the two crossgrain ends together to form a tube, offsetting edges so that one strip width extends beyond each end as shown.

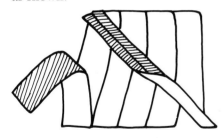

5 ▪ Cut along the marked lines to make a continuous bias strip.

Applying a Bias Binding

1 ▪ If you are using self bias, cut and press the bias strip with the tape maker as directed in the manufacturer's instructions.

2 ▪ Fold the piece lengthwise, not quite in half, so that one side extends slightly beyond the other. With purchased double-fold bias tape, re-press the center fold as above if the tape doesn't come this way.

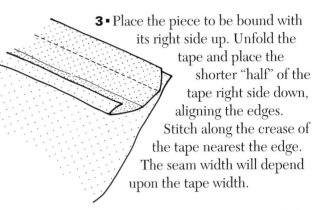

3 ▪ Place the piece to be bound with its right side up. Unfold the tape and place the shorter "half" of the tape right side down, aligning the edges. Stitch along the crease of the tape nearest the edge. The seam width will depend upon the tape width.

4 ▪ When applying a continuous binding around the outer edge of a piece, fold under approximately ½ inch (1 cm) at the end of the tape to overlap the starting point.

5 ▪ On the right side, press the tape toward the edge of the piece, taking care not to press out the creases in the tape.

6 ▪ Fold the tape over the edge of the piece so that the inner folded edge covers the first stitching line on the wrong side. Glue baste, if desired. Stitch from the right side in the ditch formed by the previous seamline, making sure to catch the folded edge of the tape on the reverse side.

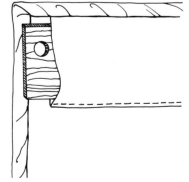

HOW OFTEN HAVE YOU BOUGHT A SPOOL OF THREAD ONLY TO FIND YOU ALREADY HAD SEVERAL OF THE SAME COLOR? *When dozens of spools are tangled together in a box, it's easier to buy a new one than to hunt through the snarl. With an organizer like this one, threads can be sorted by color and kept in plain view along with their matching bobbins. It is a handy means, too, of keeping track of small gadgets like thimbles and markers.*

Sheer Organization

designer:
Joyce Baldwin

Made to cover a heavy-duty hanger, the organizer takes up little space in a closet. And it's pretty enough to display on the sewing room wall hung from a decorative picture hanger.

The backing and pockets are made of sheer warp knit fabric that is soft and not difficult to sew. Bias binding for the edges can be purchased, or can be made from fabric to match the room's color scheme. Ribbon, to match the binding, separates the pockets and ties the hanger in place.

Dimensions

Our organizer is 18 inches (46 cm) wide and 31 inches (78.5 cm) long at center front. The size can be adjusted, of course, to suit your needs and the width of your hanger. Make the pattern first to calculate the materials you will need.

Materials

- Heavy-duty plastic or wooden hanger
- Paper or gridded pattern-drafting material
- Warp knit or other sheer fabric, approximately 2 yards (1.85 m)
- Double-fold bias tape or bias binding, approximately 6 yards (5.5 m)
- Ribbon, ¼ inch (.7 cm) wide, approximately 3 yards (2.75 m)

1
Keeping Your Tools at Hand

One of the most perplexing problems in most sewing rooms is keeping track of small notions and gadgets. Hidden away in boxes and drawers, it's easy to forget they exist. On the following pages are lots of ideas for organizing sewing supplies so they can be located easily when you need them—and stored neatly when you don't.

Construction

Detailed instructions for making and applying bias binding are on page 12.

1 ▪ Make a pattern for the back section. On paper, trace around the hanger, extending the sides straight downward to the desired length and rounding the point at the base of the hanger neck as indicated by the solid lines in the illustration. Add ¼ inch (.5 cm) seam allowance around all edges.

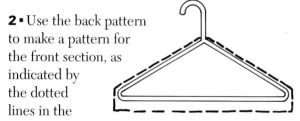

2 ▪ Use the back pattern to make a pattern for the front section, as indicated by the dotted lines in the illustration. Draw a straight line across the base of the hanger neck. Draw a line across the bottom of the hanger and add seam allowance there.

3 ▪ Cut fabric for the front and back sections. For pockets, measure the length between the lower edge of the front section and the lower edge of the back and divide by four (or to make the desired number of pocket rows). Cut fabric for each row the length of this measurement and width of the back section.

4 ▪ Bind the straight neck edge and lower edge of the front section with bias. Bind one long edge (the upper edge) of each pocket strip.

5 ▪ With wrong sides together, place front and back sections together and baste along upper edges.

6 ▪ Place the lower pocket strip on the back with wrong sides together, lower edges and sides aligned. Baste.

7 ▪ Position the next pocket strip, right sides together, above the lower pocket, with the bound edge downward and the unfinished edge approximately ⅜ inch (1 cm) above the lower pocket edge. Stitch with a zigzag stitch, overcasting the raw edge at the same time. Flip pocket upward and edgestitch close to the seamline, then again approximately ¼ inch (.7 cm) from first stitching. Baste sides of the pocket to the back along the seam allowances.

8 ▪ Attach the two remaining pocket strips in the same way.

9 ▪ Cut two lengths of ribbon to extend from the lower edge of the organizer to approximately 6 inches (15 cm) above the upper edge of the top pocket. Pin each in place to divide the pocket sections in thirds. Topstitch in place along both ribbon edges.

10 ▪ Bind outer edges of the organizer with double-fold tape or bias binding, mitering the lower corners and easing around upper curves.

11 ▪ Sew a 6-inch (15-cm) length of ribbon to the lower edge of the upper front section to correspond to each tie extension on the pockets.

12 ▪ Stitch a bow, if desired, to the upper front at the hanger neck opening.

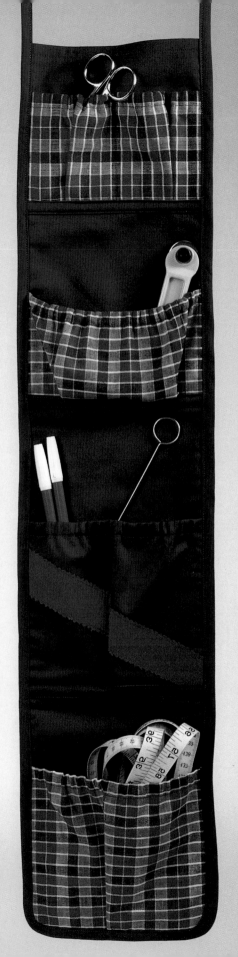

LONG, NARROW SPACES CAN OFFER STORAGE OPPORTUNITY. *Here is a gadget-holder that is designed to fit neatly into just such a spot. It goes a long way toward eliminating the clutter around the sewing machine and keeps all kinds of small essentials in perfect order. It can provide a decorative element, too, with pockets embellished with appliqué or embroidery, or cut from contrasting fabric.*

Small-Space Organizer

The pockets can be planned to suit your storage needs. These have pleats at the lower edges for roominess, and elastic across the tops to keep things in place. The pockets are sewn to the right side of the backing and the sides bound to the backing with bias that extends at the upper edges to form ties or a hanging loop. The front and back are open at the top to accommodate a piece of foamcore to keep the holder straight.

Materials

Quantities will depend upon the size of your holder. Read through the cutting instructions to determine fabric needs.

- Fabric, for front, back, pockets, and bias trim (double-fold bias tape can be used for trim and ties)

- Elastic, ¼ inch (.7 cm) wide, one piece for each pocket cut 1 inch (2.5 cm) longer than the holder width

- For lightweight fabric, one piece of fusible interfacing cut to the finished dimensions of the holder

- Foamcore or stiff poster board the size of the finished holder

Cutting

1 ▪ Determine the finished dimensions of your holder. Cut front and back to these dimensions.

2 ▪ Cut pocket sections. To the desired finished length of each, add 1½ inches (4 cm) for seam allowance and elastic casing. In width, add to the width of the holder 1 inch (2.5 cm) for an ease pleat in each pocket section.

3 ▪ Cut strips for bias binding according to the instructions on page 12. Allow enough to bind all outer edges of the holder and extend to form ties or a loop for hanging, and to stitch across all pocket sections except the lower one.

Construction

1 ▪ If lightweight fabric is used, fuse interfacing to the wrong side of the holder front section.

2 ▪ Embellish pocket sections as desired. Stitch a ½ inch (1.5 cm) double hem along one (the upper) long edge of each section.

3 ▪ Thread elastic through each pocket casing.

4 ▪ Pin pocket sections in place, right side up, on the holder front section, aligning along the sides. Align the lower edge of the bottom pocket with the lower edge of the holder. Form pleats at the lower edge of each pocket section. Pull elastic to gather pocket upper edges to fit.

5 ▪ Stitch pockets in place at the sides, stitching approximately ¼ inch (.5 cm) from the edges. seams, stitching securely across the elastic ends. Stitch across the lower edge of each section approximately ¼ inch (.5 cm) from the raw edge.

6 ▪ Press and fold bias binding with a tape maker, or unfold a length of bias tape at the center. Cut a length for each pocket except the lower one.

7 ▪ Position a strip over the lower edge of each pocket section and stitch close to both folded edges.

8 ▪ Stitch bias binding over the upper edge of the front section.

9 ▪ Press and stitch a ¾ inch (2 cm) double hem across the upper edge of the back section.

10 ▪ Place back and front sections with wrong sides together, aligning sides and lower edge. Stitch along sides and lower edge.

11 ▪ Bind the outer edges with bias, extending at the upper ends to make a loop or ties for hanging.

12 ▪ Cut the foamcore to fit and slip it into its pocket.

CARPENTERS AND COOKS WEAR APRONS TAILORED TO THEIR TASKS, AND NOW WE HAVE ONE OF OUR OWN. *The designer, a professional dressmaker, fashioned this model after years of wasting time looking for the scissors or tape measure during fittings.*

The outer pocket has a buttoned bellows pocket at the center, and is subdivided on both sides to accommodate shears, a ruler, pencils, chalk, and other necessities. The built-in pincushion is backed with stiff plastic to prevent injuries. The inner pocket is open all the way across to hold fabric or pattern pieces. The tape measure loops securely around its own holder, always where it can be located without a search.

Sewer's Apron

designer: **Elizabeth Searle**

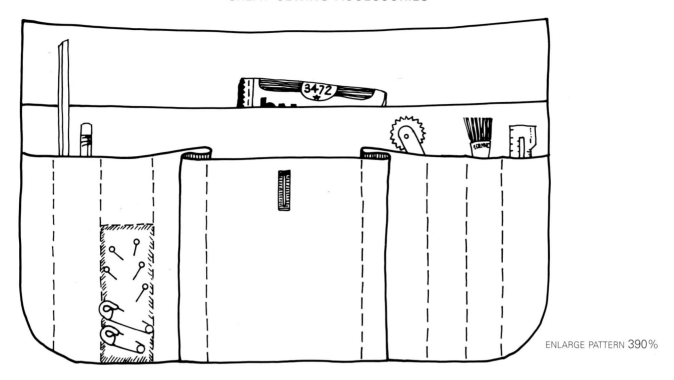

ENLARGE PATTERN 390%

Materials

- Fabric, 1¼ yards (1.15 m), 45 inches (115 cm) wide

- Large button

- Piece of stiff plastic 2¼ by 5 inches (5.75 by 12.5 cm)

- Fiberfill, wool scraps, or other stuffing for pincushion

- If self bias will not be used, you will also need 3 yards (2.75 m) extra wide double-fold bias binding.

Cutting

1 ▪ Enlarge the pattern. Cut the main section and inner pocket from fabric. For the outer pocket, cut the pattern piece in half vertically and pin to fabric with 4 inches (10 cm) between the cut edges, the top and bottom edges even. Cut the piece and mark center front.

2 ▪ For waistband and ties, cut one piece 3¼ inches (8.5 cm) wide and 61 inches (155 cm) long.

3 ▪ Cut strips to make bias binding. You will need 3 yards (2.75 m), 2½ inches (6.25 cm) wide. If you will use a bias tape maker, cut to the width instructed for finished binding ⅝ to ¾ inch (1.5 to 2 cm) wide. Detailed instructions for making and sewing bias binding are on page 12.

Construction

1 ▪ Bind the upper edges of the outer and inner pockets with bias.

2 ▪ On the outer pocket, fold and press a 1-inch (2.5-cm) pleat 4 inches (10 cm) to each side of center. Stitch close to the outer

crease on each pleat. Baste across the lower edges.

3 ▪ Work a buttonhole at center front, with the top approximately 1 inch (2.5 cm) below the pocket edge.

4 ▪ Position the outer pocket on the inner pocket, aligning sides and lower edges. Baste.

5 ▪ Mark location for the pincushion with chalk. On the model, the inner edge is approximately ½ inch (1.5 cm) from the pleat. It is 2½ inches (6.5 cm) wide, with the upper edge 5¾ inches (14.5 cm) from the apron lower edge. Stitch the sides and upper edge of the section, and stitch again approximately ¼ inch (.5 cm) outside the first stitching.

6 ▪ Remove basting at the lower edge of the pincushion and insert the plastic piece. Stuff firmly with wool or fiberfill to ½ inch (1.5 cm) from the lower edge. Baste across the lower edge.

7 ▪ Chalk mark the pocket divisions, using the photo or your own equipment needs as a guide. Make a small pocket above the pincushion by extending the stitching lines to the top of the pocket. Double stitch each pocket division, and stitch across between the two stitching lines at the top.

8 ▪ Place the pockets on the apron main section and baste around the edges.

9 ▪ For the tape measure loop, fold a 6-inch (15-cm) strip of bias and stitch the folded long edges together. Fold the piece in half, place the ends together at the apron outer edge, just above the inner pocket edge. Baste. Place the loop on the left side of the apron if you are right handed, and vice versa.

10 ▪ Bind the sides and lower edge with bias.

11 ▪ Fold under the ends of the waistband/tie piece. Press.

12 ▪ Pin the right side of the band to the apron wrong side, matching centers. Stitch, using ⅜ inch (1 cm) seam allowance.

13 ▪ Fold under and press the seam allowance on the remaining band edge. Position it on the apron right side to just cover the previous stitching; stitch close to the edge.

14 ▪ Fold under the seam allowances on the tie extensions and stitch close to the edges.

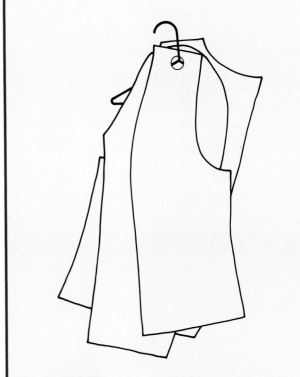

☞ TIP

Pristine Patterns

Patterns you have drafted and those you have bonded to heavier paper for durability can be kept crease-free and ready to use. Punch a hole at the top of each piece and slip it onto a clothes hanger. Put the original pattern envelope and instruction sheets into a zip-lock bag and hang it with the pattern for quick identification. Add a fabric swatch from each garment you've made from the pattern.

Lined
Basket

designer:
Joyce Baldwin

BASKETS ARE WONDERFUL, BOTH FROM AN AESTHETIC AND A PRACTICAL STANDPOINT, FOR STORING JUST ABOUT ANYTHING. *A pretty lining will prevent snags to fabrics or trims, and will keep pins or other tiny items from slipping through the cracks. A decoratively lined basket, perhaps containing one or two of the latest sewing gadgets or a handful of fat quarters, makes a thoughtful gift for a friend who sews.*

Materials

- Basket
- Fabric for lining. The lining is double thickness; you can use the same fabric for both layers or choose a complementary material for one. Commercial double-fold bias tape can be used for ties.
- Bias fabric strips or ribbon for ties

Construction

1 ▪ Place a fabric piece in the basket and push into the corners. Fabric should extend 1¼ inches (3 cm) above basket. Cut off the excess. Remove the fabric from the basket and trim neatly. Use this piece to cut a second fabric layer.

2 ▪ Place the fabrics with right sides together and stitch ¼ inch (.5 cm) from the edges. Leave an opening for turning. Turn, press, and stitch the opening.

3 ▪ Place the fabric in the basket and mark for gathering. For a rectangular basket like this one, gather around each of the corners. For a round basket, gather all the way around. Mark gathering line approximately 1 inch (2.5 cm) below the top of the basket.

4 ▪ Stitch two rows of gathering, ¼ inch (.5 cm) apart, at the marked points. Draw up bobbin threads to fit the fabric to the basket. Knot the threads securely.

5 ▪ If the lining will show through to the right side of the basket, you may wish to cover the gathering line with a fabric strip. Press under the edges of strip and edgestitch in place to cover the gathers.

6 ▪ With the lining in place, mark around the bottom where the bottom meets the sides. On the outer side of the fabric, stitch a 1⁄16 inch (2 mm) tuck along the mark.

7 ▪ Make four ties, ¼ inch (.5 cm) wide and 15 inches (38 cm) long, or cut ribbon this length.

8 ▪ Stitch the center of each tie behind the gathers at each corner of the lining, or at four points around the lining for a round basket. Thread the ties through to the outside of the basket and tie the lining in place.

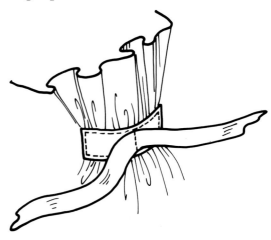

WHAT COULD BE MORE CONVENIENT? TOOLS AND SUPPLIES WITHIN REACH AT THE BACK OF THE SEWING CHAIR AND A COMFORTABLE CHAIR-BACK CUSHION TOO. *A large detachable pocket at the lower chair back holds the work in progress. Designed especially for those whose sewing space serves double duty, as a dining room perhaps, the caddy can quickly be removed and put away, keeping the project and essential tools neatly together until the next sewing session.*

Chair-Back Cushion and Caddy

designer: **Suzanne Koppi**

We have used medium-weight corduroy for the caddy, back cushion, pocket facings, and the detachable pocket. Print fabric was used for the caddy pockets, seat cushion, detachable pocket flap facing, and for the scrap can sling.

Materials

- Refer to the measuring and cutting instructions to determine fabric amounts.
- Fabric, medium to heavy weight, for caddy, back cushion, and all ties
- Contrasting fabric for seat cushion and pockets
- Pillow form for seat cushion
- Foam piece for back cushion, approximately 1½ inches (4 cm), or several layers of thick batting
- Large button or snap for the detachable pocket

Measuring and Cutting

To figure fabric needs, draw a diagram showing your chair measurements and measurements of the caddy, cushions, and pockets.

1 ▪ For the caddy, measure the width of the chair back and from the top to just below the seat. Add ½ inch (1 cm) seam allowance and cut two pieces from fabric.

2 ▪ For the back cushion, measure the chair inner back height and width. Add seam allowances and cut two pieces of fabric. Cut foam or batting to the finished dimensions of the cover.

3 ▪ For the detachable pocket, measure from the finish point of the caddy to the desired length of the pocket. Add seam allowances and cut two.

4 ▪ Make a paper pattern for the pocket flap as shown, making it the width of the pocket sections. Cut one piece from main fabric and one from contrast.

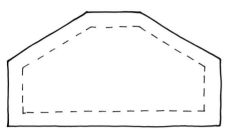

5 ▪ For the seat cushion, cut two pieces of contrast fabric the dimensions of the pillow form plus seam allowance.

6 ▪ Cut 2-inch (5-cm) fabric strips for ties. It is easiest to make long strips, then cut them to length. For the back cushion and caddy you will need eight 6-inch (15-cm) lengths; for the seat cushion, four 12-inch (30-cm) lengths; for the detachable pocket, two 12-inch (30-cm) lengths. To join the caddy and back cushion, you will need four 3-inch (7.5-cm) pieces.

7 ▪ Cut pockets and pocket facings for the caddy. Cut a main pocket and facing the width of the caddy, and to the desired height with seam allowances top and bottom. Cut facing the same size.

8 ▪ Cut the smaller rectangular pocket and facing, adding seam allowance to the desired finished measurements. (The pocket shown is 5½ by 7 inches, or 14 by 18 cm.)

9 ▪ The triangular scissors pocket shown is 4½ inches (11.5 cm) across the top and 7 inches (18 cm) in height. Add seam allowances, and cut pocket and facing.

Construction: CADDY

1 ▪ Make the ties. Fold strip(s) in half lengthwise, right side out, and press. Fold raw edges inward; press. Stitch along both long edges and cut to needed lengths. Clean finish both ends of 12-inch (30-cm) ties and one end of each 6-inch (15-cm) tie.

2 ▪ Make pockets for the caddy. For smaller rectangular pocket and triangular pocket, stitch pocket to facing with right sides together, leaving an opening for turning. Turn, and press under seam allowances at the openings. Topstitch across the upper edge then topstitch in place on the outer caddy section.

3 ▪ For the wide pocket, stitch pocket to facing, right sides together, along upper and lower edges. Turn. Topstitch across the upper edge. Baste to the caddy along the lower edge and sides.

4 ▪ Stack two 3-inch (7.5-cm) tie sections and baste them together just inside each side seam allowance at the caddy upper edge, ends aligned with the caddy edge as shown. Baste.

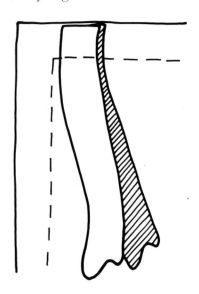

5 ▪ Position and baste two 6-inch (15-cm) ties at each lower corner, stacking them as above.

6 ▪ With right sides together, stitch the caddy sections, keeping the tie ends free. Leave a large opening across the lower edge. Turn right side out. Press under the seam allowances along the lower edge and edgestitch the opening.

Construction:
BACK CUSHION

1 • Baste two ties at each lower corner of one cover section as for the caddy.

2 • Baste the short tie ends of the caddy upper edge to the upper edge of the cushion cover section.

3 • Pin on the remaining cover piece, right sides together, with the caddy section sandwiched between and keeping tie ends free.

4 • Stitch, leaving most of the lower edge open for turning. Trim and turn right side out. Insert the batting or foam, and topstitch the opening closed.

Construction:
DETACHABLE POCKET

1 • Stitch pocket back to front, right sides together, along sides and lower edge.

2 • Press under the seam allowance on the long edge of the flap facing.

3 • Stitch flap sections with right sides together along all but the pressed edge. Turn right side out.

4 • Pin unfinished edge of the pocket flap to the pocket upper edge with right sides together. Stitch. Clip at the side seams and fold flap facing over the seamline. Stitch close to the fold.

5 • Press and stitch a narrow double hem in the remaining pocket edge.

6 • Fold two 12-inch (30-cm) ties in half. Position one at each side of the pocket back, the fold approximately ½ inch (1.5 cm) below the flap seamline. Stitch in place with an X through both tie thicknesses.

7 • Work a buttonhole at the flap point, or sew on a snap.

Construction:
SEAT CUSHION

1 • Stitch cover back to front with right sides together, leaving open along most of one edge. Trim, turn, and press under seam allowances along the opening.

2 • Insert the pillow form. Edgestitch the opening closed.

3 • Fold each 12-inch (30-cm) tie section at the halfway point to form a right angle. Position at the corner of the cushion as shown. Stitch, keeping pillow corner free if possible.

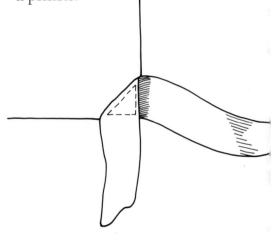

Scrap Can Sling

Keep the sewing area neat with a container in just the right place to catch trimmed threads and scraps. The sling hangs at the side of the chair and holds a three-pound coffee can. A plastic one-gallon water bottle, with the top cut away, could be substituted; adjust the pattern at the short vertical seam.

Materials

- Fabric, ¾ yard (.7 m)
- Coffee can or other container
- Decorative cord, 1 yard (1 m)

Instructions

Seam allowance is ⅜ inch (1 cm).

1 ▪ Enlarge or copy pattern to size. Cut from doubled fabric.

2 ▪ Stitch pieces, right sides together, along short vertical side. Clean finish seam allowances to within 1 inch (2.5 cm) of bottom. Clip seam allowance and press open that section of seam.

3 ▪ Check fit around the container and stitch the long vertical side to 4 inches (10 cm) from the upper edges. Clean finish seam allowances.

4 ▪ Stitch across the short upper edges; press the seam open.

5 ▪ Hem the seam allowances around the open upper end of the seam with a narrow double hem. Reinforce stitch across the seamline at the lower end of the opening.

6 ▪ Press and stitch a narrow double hem around the curved edge.

7 ▪ Make a casing at the unfinished lower edge. Turn under ¾ inch (2 cm) and press. Turn in the raw edge ¼ inch (.5 cm); press. Stitch close to the edge. Open up the short vertical seam along the inner casing to insert the cord.

8 ▪ Put the container in place and draw up the cord to fit.

ENLARGE PATTERN 550%

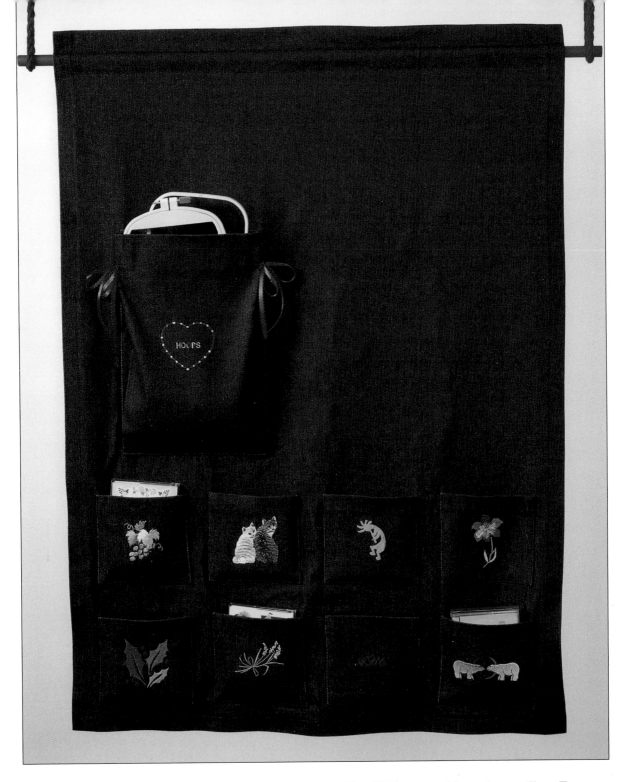

Organized Embroidery

designers: **Beth Hill and Judith Robertson**
construction: **Beth Hill**

Organized Embroidery

THE NEW EMBROIDERY MACHINES PRESENT A SPECIAL STORAGE PROBLEM: HOW TO KEEP TRACK OF ALL THE DESIGN CARDS. *Rather than hiding them away in a drawer, this designer has opted for a wall organizer that is a work of art in itself. Each pocket is embroidered with a motif from the card package stored inside. A large expandable pocket holds three hoops. Notice there is room for future additions to the collection; the pockets are all cut out, ready to embroider appropriately and stitch in place.*

On this organizer, the upper hem forms a casing for a painted dowel. For other ways to hang it, see page 10. The finished organizer is 29 inches (73.5 cm) wide and 40 inches (101.5 cm) long.

Materials

- For the backing, medium to heavy fabric 46 inches (112 cm) long and 33 inches (84 cm) wide
- For the pockets, the same or a complementary fabric. See instructions for sizes
- Interfacing, medium weight for the backing; for the pockets, use the weight needed to back the embroidery
- Narrow ribbon, 1 yard (1 m)
- Dowel, ⁹⁄₁₆ inch (1.5 cm) diameter, 34 inches (86 cm) long

Construction: MAIN SECTION

1 ▪ Fuse interfacing to the large fabric piece. Clean finish the upper edge. Press a 1-inch (2.5 cm) hem at each side and across the lower edge, mitering the corners. Stitch.

2 ▪ Fold the upper edge 3 inches (7.5 cm) to the wrong side. Stitch ¼ inch (.5 cm) from the edge. To form rod pocket, stitch again 1½ inches (4 cm) above the first stitching, or as needed to accommodate dowel.

3 ▪ Mark pocket positions on the backing. Finished size of the hoop pocket is 8½ inches (21½ cm) wide and 12½ inches (32 cm) long; the card pockets are 5½ inches (14 cm) wide and 5 inches (12.5 cm) long.

Construction: HOOP POCKET

1 ▪ Cut fabric 13½ inches (34 cm) wide and 14 inches (36 cm) long. Fuse interfacing to the wrong side. Clean finish all edges.

2 ▪ Fold the upper edge 1 inch (2.5 cm) to the right side of the pocket. Stitch the ends with ½ inch (1 cm) seam allowance. Trim, turn right side out, and press. Stitch the hem in place.

3 ▪ Fold under ½ inch (1 cm) seam allowance on sides; press.

4 ▪ Make a pleat at each side. Crease the fabric 2 inches (5 cm) in from each side and bring the crease even with the side folded edge. Press. Baste the pleats in place along the lower edge seam allowance.

5 ▪ Embroider the pocket as you wish.

6 ▪ Cut ribbon into four pieces. Pin a piece at the hemline under each side of the pocket, ribbon end even with the pocket inner edge.

7 ▪ Fold under one end of each remaining ribbon and stitch it just under the crease of each pleat, opposite the other ribbons.

8 ▪ Fold under the seam allowance at the lower edge; press.

9 ▪ Topstitch the pocket in place, stitching close to the edge. Stitch the sides first, then across the bottom.

Construction: CARD POCKETS

It is easiest to fuse interfacing to the fabric piece before cutting individual pockets.

1 ▪ Cut a 6½ inch square for each pocket. Clean finish all edges.

2 ▪ Hem the upper edge of each pocket as for the hoop pocket.

3 ▪ Press sides and lower edge ½ inch (1 cm) to the wrong side, mitering the corners.

4 ▪ Embroider the pockets and topstitch them in place.

LIKE THOSE DESIGNED FOR FISHERMEN AND PHOTOGRAPHERS, THIS VEST IS MEANT TO KEEP NECESSARY GEAR IN ITS PROPER PLACE. *Unlike those others, it is cleverly decorated to suit the sewer's desire to embellish. The sunflower center is a handy pincushion. The birdhouse "door" is the opening for a small pocket, just the right size for tailor's chalk or another small object. Full-width pockets across the lower front are faced with lining fabric, and can be subdivided to accommodate your own equipment.*

A Sewer's Vest

designer:
Suzanne Koppi

Any vest pattern with traditional front points and without darts can be used as the basis for this one. If the pattern has facings, eliminate them and cut a full lining from the vest pattern. We chose cotton chambray for the outer vest and lined it with cozy plaid flannel.

Materials

- Fabric for vest and lining, according to pattern, plus an additional ⅜ yard (.35 m) of each for pockets

- Fabric scraps for birdhouse and roof, and for sunflower center

- Yellow rattail cord for sunflower petals, 3 yards (2.75 m)

- Brown double fold bias tape, 1 yard (1 m)

- Green ribbon, 1½ inches (4 cm) wide, ½ yard (.5 m)

- White ribbon, ¼ inch (.7 cm) wide, 2 yards (1.85 m)

- Blackbird button

- 2 sunflower buttons

- Fiberfill or cotton balls for pincushion stuffing

Cutting

1 ▪ Cut the vest and lining according to the vest pattern.

2 ▪ For the front pockets, mark the desired upper pocket edge on the front pattern piece and draw a line across the pattern piece at a right angle to the center front line. Add seam allowance above this line to establish the cutting line. Cut two pockets and two lining pieces.

3 ▪ For the birdhouse and facing, cut two pieces 5 inches (12.5 cm) wide and 3¼ inches (8.5 cm) high.

4 ▪ For the birdhouse roof, cut a triangle approximately 6 inches (15 cm) wide at the base and 3 inches (7.5 cm) high.

5 ▪ For the sunflower center, cut a circle 4 inches (10 cm) in diameter.

Pockets and Embellishment

1 ▪ Using the photo as a guide, position lengths of ribbon on one pocket section to make the fence. Stitch in place, stitching close to both edges of the ribbon. On the other pocket section, mark the position of the birdhouse pole. Press open the center crease in a length of bias binding and stitch it in place along both edges.

2 ▪ Stitch each lower pocket section to a lining section across the upper edge with right sides together. Turn, press, and topstitch. Position pockets on the vest front pieces and chalk mark the pocket upper edges on the vest fronts. Remove the pockets.

3 ▪ For the birdhouse, place the fabric rectangles with right sides together and draw an oval approximately 2 inches (5 cm) long near the center. Stitch around the oval using a short stitch length. Cut out the oval, cutting close to the stitching. Turn right side out and press. Baste sections together around the edges, stitching ¼ inch (.5 cm) from the edges. Fold under the sides and lower edge along the stitching; press.

4 ▪ Fold under ¼ inch (.5 cm) around the edges of the roof section. Press.

5 ▪ Position the house on the vest and position the roof to overlap the house upper edge. Cut a length of bias binding for the upper part of the pole, extending it 1 inch (2.5 cm) or so below the pocket placement line. Press open the center fold. Slip the upper end under the house. Topstitch the house, roof, and pole in place, stitching close to all edges.

6 ▪ Stitch a folded length of rattail cord in place for the blackbird's perch, and sew on the button.

7 ▪ For the sunflower center, machine baste ¼ inch (.5 cm) from the edge of the fabric circle. Pull the bobbin thread to draw up slightly, and press under the edge at the stitching line.

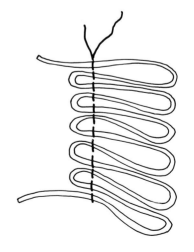

8 ▪ For the flower petals, fold the rattail cord and stitch it as shown, making the loops approximately 1½ inches (4 cm) long. Stitch enough length to surround the flower center.

9 ▪ Position the flower center on the vest front and slip the cord petals under the edge. Topstitch in place close to the edge of the center circle, leaving an opening at the bottom for stuffing.

10 ▪ Cut a length of bias binding for the stem. Press open the center crease and position it with the upper end under the opening of the flower center. Stitch along both edges. Stuff the center firmly and stitch the opening.

11 ▪ Cut lengths of green ribbon for the leaves. Turn under the upper corners of each leaf, and stitch them in place.

12 ▪ Pin pocket sections in place on the vest front. Baste inside the seam allowance.

13 ▪ Stitch vertical divisions as you require.

Vest Construction

1 ▪ Right sides together, stitch vest fronts to back at shoulders. Stitch lining sections the same way.

2 ▪ Stitch the vest to the lining at the front edges and neck, around the armholes, and across the lower back. Don't stitch the side seams yet. Trim seam allowances and press.

3 ▪ Turn right side out by pulling both lower front points through the same back side seam opening.

4 ▪ Stitch the side seams. Pin the outer vest front to back at the side, matching the armhole and lower edge seamlines. Stitch, extending stitching as far into the lining as possible. Press under the remaining lining seam allowances and whipstitch closed.

5 ▪ To keep the lining from rolling to the outside, topstitch around the neckline, along the front and lower edges, and around the armholes.

6 ▪ Sew on the buttons. Work buttonholes if desired.

Heart in Hand Chatelaine

designer: **Terry Taylor**

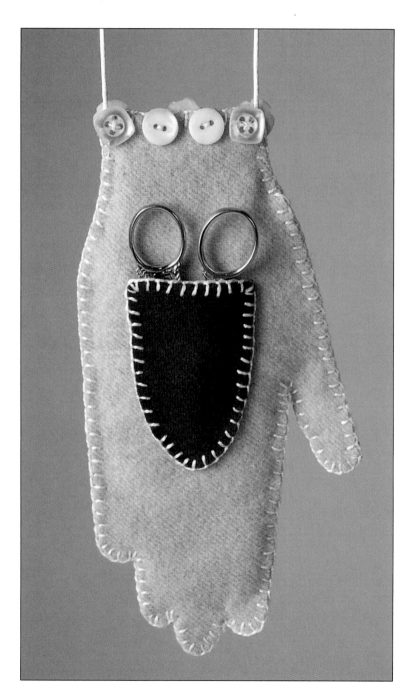

GIVE A FRIEND A HELPING HAND!
A scaled-down chatelaine holds the sewing essentials: a few pins and needles in the pincushion heart on one side, and the smallest scissors in their own pocket on the other side. This project provides a wonderful opportunity to use up scraps of wool or felt, too.

Materials

- Wool or felt for the background
- Wool or felt scrap for the heart
- Pearl cotton or embroidery floss to match or contrast
- Stuffing: wool roving or cotton balls
- Thin cardboard, 8-inch (20-cm) square
- Decorative cord or ribbon, 1 yard (1 m)
- Buttons or charms for embellishment

Construction

1 ▪ Enlarge and copy the hand and heart patterns and cut them out. Transfer the hand pattern to the cardboard and cut out.

2 ▪ Cut the hand from doubled fabric. Double the flesh-colored wool. Cut one heart from fabric.

3 ▪ Pin the heart in place on the right side of one of the hand sections.

2
Needles and Pins

The ubiquitous red tomato with its attached emery strawberry has been around for as long as most of us can remember. It is respected and highly serviceable, but there are alternatives to the tradition. In this section are some most unusual—and just as functional—alternatives. Any one of them will make a thoughtful and practical gift for a sewing friend who may be inspired to return the favor some day.

ENLARGE PATTERN 132%

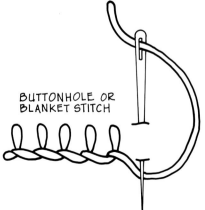

BUTTONHOLE OR
BLANKET STITCH

4 ▪ Stitch it in place with floss, using small buttonhole stitches.

5 ▪ Make a small slit on the reverse side of the hand under the heart. Stuff, then stitch the opening closed.

6 ▪ Cut a small rectangle of fabric large enough to accommodate the blades of a small pair of embroidery scissors. Round off the corners at one end as shown in the photo. Pin it to the right side of the other hand section. Stitch it to the hand with small blanket stitches.

7 ▪ Trim away ¼ inch (.5 cm) around all edges of the cardboard hand. (Don't worry about neatness; it will be encased between the fabric layers.)

8 ▪ Align the hands with wrong sides together and pin them to prevent slipping.

9 ▪ Start at one wrist corner and use small buttonhole stitches to join the two layers. Work to the opposite wrist corner, leaving the straight edge open.

10 ▪ Slip the cardboard hand inside, trimming if needed to fit.

11 ▪ Cut cord or ribbon to a length that will allow it to slip easily over your head. Pin each end between the hand layers at the wrist. Stitch securely in place with tiny stitches.

12 ▪ Finish off the wrist edge with buttonhole stitches.

13 ▪ Sew buttons or charms across the wrist to embellish the chatelaine.

Felt Needle Books and Pincushions

designer: **Dale Liles**

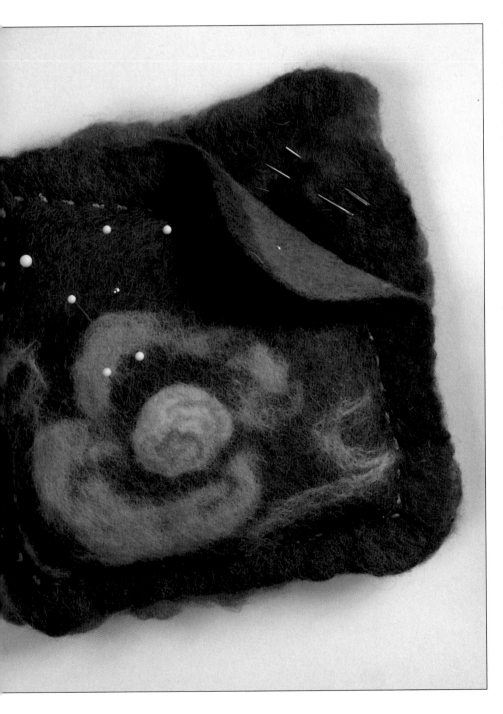

WOOL FELT IS AN IDEAL MEDIUM FOR A PINCUSHION. *Because the material is not woven, there are no tough threads to interfere with the needle or pin piercing the fabric, and the felt will not exhibit puncture wounds after a period of use.*

Wool felt is difficult to locate, but it is not the least bit difficult to make. Commercial crafters' felt is usually acrylic fiber. It is of even thickness, tougher and less pliable than wool, and not as good a bet for this project. When you make your own felt you can add design and color, and you can regulate the thickness as needed.

Double-layer Needle Book and Pincushion

For a beginning felter, this design is the simplest.

Materials

- Felt-making materials
- Embroidery floss or pearl cotton for stitching
- Stuffing: wool fleece, leftover bits of felt, or scraps of wool fabric cut finely

Construction

1 ▪ Make two pieces of felt, approximately 8 inches (20 cm) square.

2 ▪ Using several strands of embroidery floss, stitch the pieces together along two adjacent corners, using small stitches and sewing approximately ¾ inch (2 cm) from the raw edges.

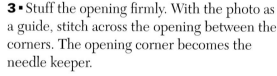

3 ▪ Stuff the opening firmly. With the photo as a guide, stitch across the opening between the corners. The opening corner becomes the needle keeper.

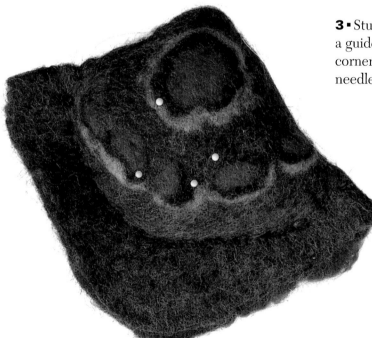

Round Pincushion

The small felt ball has a ribbon attached so it can be hung conveniently on the unused spool holder of the sewing machine to catch a wandering pin or hold an extra machine needle.

Materials

- Felt-making supplies, with bits of yarn or colored fleece to add color
- Narrow ribbon, approximately ½ yard (.5 m)
- Two beads

Construction

1 • Roll bits of carded fleece into a ball, incorporating additional colors if desired.

2 • Put the ball into the toe of an old nylon stocking and knot the stocking tightly, close to the ball.

3 • Wash and dry in the machine —perhaps with a load of towels.

4 • Fold ribbon in half and thread the folded end through a tapestry or darning needle. Stitch through the center of the ball. Thread a bead onto each end of the ribbon and knot the ribbon to hold the bead in place.

Making Felt

Carded wool, or sliver, or wool batts can be found at well-stocked crafts supply stores or from mail-order suppliers that cater to spinners. For felt-making, do not use wool that is labeled "superwash;" its felting qualities have been removed. Good wool for felting comes from Merino, Romney, Lincoln, and many other breeds of sheep. Wool from the Down breeds—Hampshire and Suffolk, for example— does not felt well.

Color and design can be added when the wool is laid out to make the felt. Add bits of colored fleece at random, or add small bits of collected wool and fuzzy yarn ends.

The steps below give a very brief description of the felt-making process. Once you have tried a pincushion or needle book, you may find you are fascinated by the craft—and the fabric itself—and wish to pursue the craft. There are several good books available that provide excellent, detailed instructions for felt-making.

1 • Cover a work surface with plastic. Arrange a thin layer of fibers to cover an area slightly larger than the desired finished size of the felt.

2 • Add another layer, placing the fibers at right angles to those in the first layer.

3 • Add another five or six layers this way, incorporating other colors or yarn strands as desired.

4 • Baste through the layers an inch (2.5 cm) or so from the edge to hold them together.

5 • Wet the wool with hot water to which a little soap has been added. Gently massage the piece for several minutes to encourage the fibers to interlock. Repeat several times. For good results, use a washboard or similar bumpy surface for this step.

6 • Carefully rinse the piece then fold it in several thicknesses of toweling to remove the excess water. Let it dry completely.

Needlepoint Pincushion

designer: **Nell Paulk**

FOR HAND NEEDLEWORK, A PINCUSHION IS SO SMALL THAT IT CAN BE COMPLETED IN NEXT TO NO TIME. *Here is a sewer's dream project—it affords a way to experiment with design ideas and new techniques and to create a unique gift at the same time.*

Needlepoint for this pincushion was worked on 13-mesh natural bargello canvas with two strands of Persian wool in seven colors. Different patterns were used for the front and the back, both incorporating bargello and basket weave stitches. To finish the edges, triple strands of yarn were braided then stitched into place with yarn. Assorted tassels decorate the braided hanger loop.

Materials

- Bargello canvas, two pieces 6 by 8 inches (15 by 20 cm)
- Persian yarn in assorted colors
- Wool scraps or yarn ends for stuffing

Construction

1 ▪ Work needlepoint designs for the front and back, leaving approximately ½ inch (1 cm) border around the edges for seam allowance. Block the pieces.

2 ▪ Steam and press under the seam allowances, clipping at corners. Stitch the back and front together with a machine zigzag stitch or by hand, leaving an opening.

3 ▪ Stuff the cushion with yarn ends or finely cut wool scraps. Serger trimmings are excellent for this. Close the opening.

4 ▪ Braid triple strands of yarn to make enough length to surround the perimeter of the pincushion and extend approximately 12 inches (30 cm) so you can add tassels and make a loop for hanging.

5 ▪ With a strand of yarn, begin at one corner and sew the braid in place around the cushion.

6 ▪ Fold the braid extension to form a loop. Tie yarn tightly around the braid just below the loop. Un-braid below the loop and knot the ends of the colors separately to make the tassels.

Tassel

1 • Make a large, firm knot at one end of the cord or braid to which the tassel will be attached.

2 • Use a piece of stiff cardboard about ½ inch (1.5 cm) longer than the desired finished length of the tassel. Wrap yarn around the cardboard. The more yarn, the fuller the tassel will be.

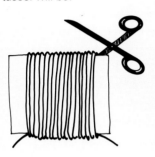

3 • Cut through the yarn along one edge of the cardboard. Hold the yarn strands at the center, and arrange them around the knot at the end of the cord to which the tassel will be attached, keeping the knot just below the midpoints of the yarn strands.

4 • Tie the bundle securely around the center, just above the knot, with a strong thread. Smooth the upper yarn ends downward over the knot.

5 • Wrap yarn tightly around all strands at the "neck" of the tassel, just below the knot. Decorate the neck area with French knots as shown, or contrast yarn, or whatever takes your fancy.

French Knots

Use a single strand of yarn for a smaller knot, a double strand to make it larger.

1 • Bring the needle out at point A.

2 • Hold the yarn taut with your other hand and twist the needle twice around the yarn.

3 • Continue to hold the thread taut and insert just the point of the needle close to A.

4 • Work the wrapped yarn down the needle to the eye end, hold it in place with a thumbnail, and push the needle on through.

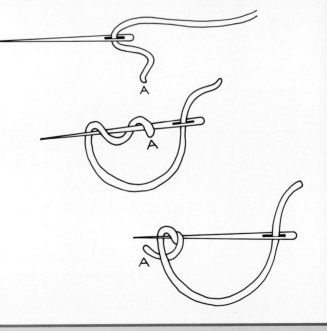

TODAY'S FABRICS, THREADS, AND SEWING TECHNIQUES REQUIRE QUITE AN ASSORTMENT OF NEEDLE SIZES AND POINT STYLES. *When a needle has been used for just a short time, we can't bear to discard it, yet we don't want to return it to the box either. It's not always easy to read the number stamped on the needle shaft, and using the wrong needle for a sewing job can produce a calamity.*

Here is an easy way to keep slightly used needles separated and identified. Use a permanent fabric marking pen to label each section of the holder as to size and needle type, or machine embroider the information before assembling the case.

This case was made up of scraps of soft silk noil, with an inner layer of thick wool. (In humid climates, polyester can encourage rust.) Open, it is 7 inches (18 cm) long and 3½ inches (9 cm) high.

Machine Needle Keeper

Materials

- Fabric scraps, for the inner case
- Fabric piece for the outer case and ties
- Wool fabric for the interlining
- Scraps of yarn, narrow ribbons, or narrow strips of fabric for ties

Construction

1 ▪ For the outer case section, cut fabric 8 inches by 4½ inches (20 cm by 11 cm). Cut interlining the same size.

2 ▪ For the ties, cut ribbons, fabric strips, or yarn into 20-inch (51-cm) lengths. Braid them together and knot the ends.

3 ▪ Piece fabrics for the inner case and trim to the size of the outer case section. Machine embroider, if desired, using a backing for stability. Baste the underlining to the wrong side.

4 ▪ Stitch the center of the tie to the center of the back.

5 ▪ With right sides together, stitch back to front, using ½ inch (1 cm) seam allowance and leaving an opening for turning. Take care to keep the cords free of the seam. Turn, press, and press under the seam allowances across the opening.

6 ▪ Topstitch close to the outer edges.

THE SEWING ROOM CAN BE A DANGEROUS PLACE FOR KIDS. *When this designer's children were toddlers she devised a combination wall caddy and ironing board stabilizer to lessen the danger of an overturned board and to eliminate the temptation of the electrical outlet behind it.*

Ironing Board Safety

designer: **Laura Rohde**

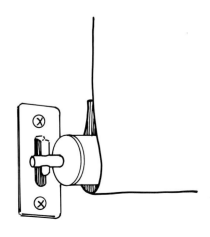

Clear vinyl pockets—placed so the kids can't reach them until they are big enough to understand the meaning of No!—keep the ironing essentials off the board. A strategically placed buttonhole accommodates the cord, and sturdy ties around the legs keep the ironing board upright.

Although the model in the photo doesn't show this feature, the caddy illustrate be attached at the lower edge too. A sash rod could be used, slipped through the lower hem and secured in brackets attached to the baseboard.

For additional stability, widen the side hems to form casings, stitch across the lower edges of the hems, and insert ⅜-inch (1-cm) dowels.

3
Practical Solutions

Sewers by nature are marvelously inventive, but not always very patient. Every sewing project seems to call for some special tool or gadget that may or may not be found in any notions department. Many of the items now offered through mail order notions suppliers' catalogs probably were invented by desperate sewers who, stalled mid-project, decided a bit of engineering was preferable to a potentially unsuccessful trip to the mall. Many times an objective look at the kitchen equipment or a prowl through the garage will turn up the perfect solution to a sewing room quandary.

Materials

- Yardage will depend upon your measurements

- Sturdy fabric. To make the caddy as wide as the ironing board length, use fabric 54 or 60 inches (137 or 152 cm) wide.

- Vinyl for pockets, 12 by 36 inches (30 by 91 cm), or as desired

- Double-fold bias tape, extra wide, 4 yards (3.7 m)

- Flexible fabric adhesive

- Heavy twill tape, 2 yards (1.85 m), for ties

Construction

1 ▪ The caddy should be hung very securely. (See page 9 for options.) Attach to the wall any hardware that will be used for hanging, then measure for fabric. Add for generous double hems at the upper and lower edges.

2 ▪ Hem the upper edge. Hang the fabric in place temporarily. Place the ironing board in front of it, several inches out from the wall.

3 ▪ Mark the hemline at the lower edge. Mark placement of the pocket lower edge at a point several inches above the top of the iron as it sits on the board. Mark the position of the button-hole, just below the top of the ironing board and toward the square end. Mark placement points for the ties behind each leg, a few inches below the top of the board.

4 ▪ Remove the fabric and hem the lower edge. Hem the sides with 1-inch (2.5-cm) double hems (wider for dowel casings). Draw a line across at the marked point for the pocket lower edge.

5 ▪ At the marked position, make a buttonhole large enough to accommodate the iron plug. Reinforce behind it with a scrap of interfacing, and/or reinforce on the front with a fabric scrap.

6 ▪ Prepare the pocket. Lay the vinyl on a protected surface. With a china marker, draw two vertical lines for the pocket divisions. Cut two 12-inch (30-cm) strips of bias, open up the center crease, and glue over the marked lines. Using adhesive, bind all edges with the bias, mitering the corners.

7 ▪ Using a number 11/75 needle and long stitches, stitch binding in place across just the upper edge.

8 ▪ Position the pocket along the marked line on the fabric and pin just through the binding to hold it in place.

9 ▪ Stitch along both edges of each bias strip. Reinforce the upper corners of the pockets.

10 ▪ Cut the twill tape in two. Center a strip over each marked point on the fabric and stitch with an X to hold it securely.

The Pressing Brick

ACHIEVING A GOOD PRESS ON WOOL IS TRICKY. *Wool and other crease-resistant fabrics require just the right combination of heat, moisture, and pressure. A modern lightweight iron just can't do the job alone.*

A common brick, wrapped tightly with wool fabric, provides enough weight to press seams flat without your having to bear down. It also allows you to direct the pressure exactly where you want it. Use a long corner to press just the seamline itself, preventing the seam edges making marks that will be visible on the right side. The short corners work well in small spaces. The flat side is good for flattening lapel and collar points, pockets, and the like.

For good tips on pressing wool successfully, see page 51.

Materials

- Brick: a clean, solid one with sharp edges
- Wool fabric, a firmly woven piece with little nap, such as flannel

Construction

Wrap the fabric very tightly around the length of the brick. Sew it securely in place by hand along the length.

Fold fabric under at each end of the brick, clipping the under layers to reduce bulk. Stitch tightly.

Note: This project is guaranteed to dull the point of your needle! Throw it away before it has the chance to damage the next delicate fabric you sew.

THE DESIGNER, A PROFESSIONAL DRESSMAKER AND EXPERT TAILOR, LISTS THIS AS HER MOST VALUABLE PRESSING AID. *It provides the weight and flexibility necessary to achieve a good press with crease-resistant fabrics like wool gabardine. It is especially useful with the curved seams at hiplines and elbows, and for darts.*

Buckshot Bag Pressing Accessory

Designer: **Marion Mulford**

The finished size of this bag is approximately 6 by 10 inches (15 by 25 cm). A smaller size can be handy, too. Very small bags, made as 1-inch (2.5-cm) to 2-inch (5-cm) squares or circles, are useful as pattern weights with fabrics easily marked or distorted by pinning.

Materials

- All-cotton muslin, for inner bag, approximately 5½ inches (14 cm) by 10 inches (25.5 cm)
- Fabric, 100 percent wool, approximately 6 by 10 inches (15 by 25 cm) for outer bag
- Buckshot, approximately 5 pounds. Buckshot is available at gunsmith shops.

Construction

1 ▪ Fold the muslin in half lengthwise. Using very short stitches, sew long edge and across one end with ¼ inch (.5 cm) seam allowance.

2 ▪ Fill the bag with the buckshot, shake it toward the stitched end, and sew the open end closed.

3 ▪ Fold the wool around the filled bag. Stitch closed, using a serger or sewing machine set at a short stitch length. Take care to keep shot pushed aside to accommodate the presser foot.

How To Use the Buckshot Bag

The bag is especially helpful for pressing darts and other curved seams. To press a dart, position it, wrong side up, over the appropriately curved section of a pressing ham. Place a strip of brown paper under the dart fold to prevent a ridge that will show on the right side of the garment. Place a piece of lightweight wool (wool prevents shine) over all, then a treated pressing cloth over that.

Apply moisture with a sponge or wet washcloth only on the area which is to be pressed. With a dry iron set for wool, press moisture into the garment fabric. Remove the pressing cloths and immediately place the buckshot bag over the dampened area, spreading the shot evenly. Keep the bag in place until the fabric is cool.

Today's irons produce quite a volume of steam, and can moisten parts of the garment not intended to be steamed, possibly causing shrinkage. The use of a dry iron, with the application of moisture only in the area to be pressed, will result in a more professional-looking garment.

IT MAY NOT BE BEAUTIFUL, BUT ONCE YOU'VE TRIED IT, YOU MIGHT ADD IT TO YOUR LIST OF MOST USEFUL POSSESSIONS. *Unfinished wood allows a good firm press, especially with recalcitrant fabrics like gabardine. The long dowel fits easily into a sleeve or pants leg to isolate the seam and its curved surface helps prevent the seam edges marking the right side of the fabric.*

Pressing Rod

Designer: **Pat Scheible**

Construction

Buy a length of hardwood dowel, 1½ to 2 inches (4 to 5 cm) in diameter and approximately 30 inches (76 cm) long. If you don't have the saw to do the job, ask the store to trim it flat along one side so it won't roll.

Another option is to use a section of unfinished handrail. It has a flat side or pre-cut groove along the length.

The rod is best left unfinished. Simply smooth off the rough places with fine sandpaper, and you will have a tool that's good for a lifetime.

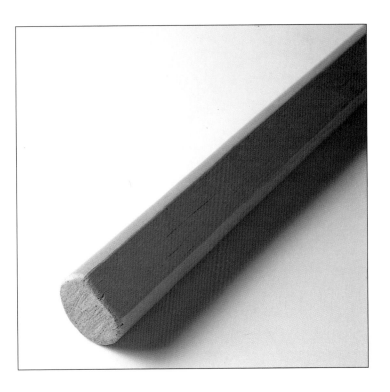

HERE IS HELP FOR SEWERS WHO BUY CORDING, LACE, AND ELASTIC ON LARGE SPOOLS OR REELS. *When lace or elastic is fed from a cardboard spool that is standing on end, twisting invariably occurs. This handy device holds the reel so the cord will feed smoothly, without a single kink. Add a pair of C-clamps to keep the holder firmly in place at the back of the sewing table.*

designer: **Laura Rohde**

Reel Holder

Materials

- Piece of ½-inch (1.3-cm) board, 4 inches (10 cm) by 18 inches (46 cm)
- Hardwood dowel, ⅜ inch (1 cm) diameter, two 12-inch (30-cm) pieces and one at 20 inches (51 cm)
- 2 screw eyes, ½ inch (1.3 cm) diameter
- White glue or carpenter's glue
- Optional materials for embellishment and finishing
- Decorative cotton cord, approximately 1 yard (1 m)
- Acrylic paints
- Polyurethane or acrylic clear finish

Tools

- Drill, with ⁵⁄₃₂-inch (4-mm) and ⅜-inch (1-cm) bits

Construction

1 ▪ With the smaller bit, drill a pilot hole at the center of one end (the upper end) of each 12-inch (30-cm) dowel. Insert a screw eye in each.

2 ▪ Spread glue around the upper 1 inch (2.5 cm) of each dowel. Wrap tightly with decorative cord. When dry, finish, if desired, with polyurethane.

3 ▪ Mark for dowel placement approximately 1 inch (2.5 cm) from each end of the board and halfway between the sides. Drill a ⅜-inch (1-cm) hole through the board at each marked position.

4 ▪ Paint designs on the board if you wish. Coat with polyurethane, if desired, after paint has dried.

5 ▪ Spread a drop or two of glue around the inside each hole and insert the dowels, fitting them tightly and checking that they are straight.

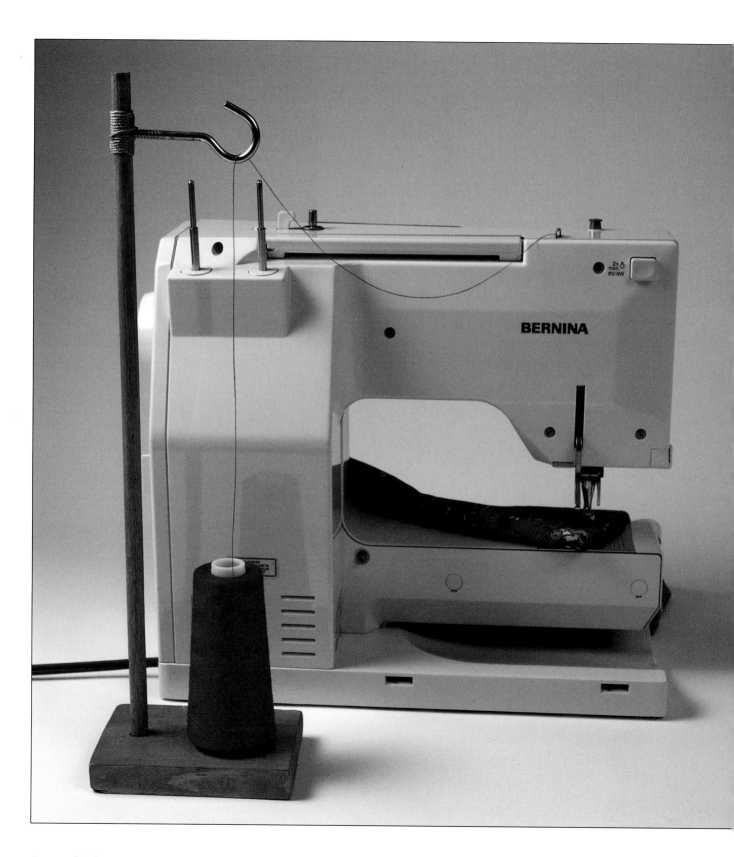

KEEP AN ECONOMICAL CONE OF THREAD IN PLACE FOR USE ON THE SEWING MACHINE. *The thread guide helps prevent snarls and tangles. For added stability, secure it to the back of the sewing table with a C-clamp.*

Thread Cone Holder

designer: **Laura Rohde**

Materials

- Piece of ½-inch (1.3-cm) board, 4 inches (10 cm) wide and approximately 5 inches (13 cm) long
- Hardwood dowel, ⅜ inch (1 cm) diameter, one 4-inch (10 cm) length and one 16 inches (40 cm)
- Ceiling hook, no. 6
- White glue or carpenter's glue
- Optional materials for embellishment and finishing
- Decorative cotton cord, approximately ½ yard (.5 m)
- Acrylic paints
- Polyurethane or acrylic clear finish

Tools

- Drill, with ⁵⁄₃₂-inch (4-mm) and ⅜-inch (1-cm) bits

Construction

1 ▪ With the smaller bit, drill a hole through the longer dowel approximately 1¼ inches (3 cm) from one end. Insert the hook, turning it so the open side is toward the short end of the dowel.

2 ▪ If desired, spread glue around the dowel approximately ¾ inch (2 cm) to either side of the hook and wrap tightly with decorative cord. Clear finish both dowels if you wish.

3 ▪ Use a cone of thread to mark the position of the shorter dowel on the board. Center the mark between the sides. Make a second mark the same distance from the other end. With the larger bit, drill a hole through the board at each marked position.

4 ▪ Paint decorations on the board if desired. Apply clear finish when the paint has dried completely.

5 ▪ Spread a drop of glue around the inside of each hole and fit the dowels in place.

REVERSIBLE FOR VARIETY AND TAILORED TO PERFECTION,
these covers are quilted with batting between the fabric layers to give them a smooth fit with no sagging. Work the quilting with matching thread in a simple pattern, or try free-motion stitching with contrasting thread.

Reversible Sewing Machine and Serger Covers

designer: **Joyce Baldwin**

4
Classy Cover-Ups

Most of us who sew treasure our machines above anything else we possess. Fine equipment deserves the best of care—including a cover to keep it free of dust when it's not in use. The designs for sewing machine and serger accessories on the following pages may include just the one you have been looking for, or may inspire you to create a unique cover or two for your own machines.

Sewing Machine Cover

The design is very simple and will accommodate most sewing machine shapes. A single central panel makes up the cover front, top, and back. Both end sections are the same size.

Materials

- Draft the pattern to determine the amount of fabric you will need.
- Gridded pattern drafting material
- Fabric for outer cover
- Fabric for lining and bias binding
- Fusible fleece

Making the Pattern

1 ▪ Measure the machine from end to end at the widest point. Measure the greatest depth across the top. Measure the height from the desired finished length of the cover. Use these measurements to draw the pattern for the central section, then add ¼ inch (1 cm) for seam allowances. Do not add hem allowance.

2 ▪ Measure the length at the ends. Measure the width across both ends; use the greater width, if applicable, to make the pattern piece. Add ¼ inch (1 cm) seam allowance.

3 ▪ Cut out the pattern pieces and pin baste them together. Try on the machine to check fit. Keep in mind that the seam allowances will be bulky and the quilted layers will be thick; adjust the pattern if necessary.

Construction

Remember to preshrink the fabrics if you plan to wash the cover.

1 ▪ Cut the central panel and two ends from outer fabric, lining, and fleece, adding approximately 1 inch (2.5 cm) around all edges. The pieces will be trimmed to size after they are quilted.

2 ▪ Cut bias strips for a finished binding approximately ½ inch (1.5 cm) wide. Cut enough length to bind seams and the lower edge. Complete instructions for making and applying bias binding are on page 12.

3 ▪ Fuse fleece to the wrong side of each outer fabric section.

4 ▪ Place wrong side of each lining section against the fleece and pin at close intervals.

5 ▪ Quilt the layers together according to your chosen design.

6 ▪ Pin the pattern to each section and trim away the excess.

7 ▪ Sew the end sections to the central panel with right sides together.

8 ▪ Bind the seams with bias, mitering the upper corners. Bind the lower edge.

Serger Cover

A single central panel makes up the front, top, and back of the cover. There is a separate piece at each end.

Materials

- Yardage will depend upon the size of your machine. Draft the pattern to determine fabric needs.
- Gridded pattern drafting material
- Fabric for outer cover
- Fabric for lining and bias binding
- Fusible fleece

Making the Pattern

1 ▪ The plastic cover normally supplied with a serger provides a readily available pattern for the new fabric cover. If your original cover is long gone, measure the machine itself. Allow for the tension knobs and other protuberances. For the central piece, measure from the front lower edge, over the top, to the back lower edge.

2 ▪ Draw the central and end pieces on the pattern material. Add ¼ inch (1 cm) seam allowances, but don't add hem allowance.

3 ▪ Cut out the pattern pieces. Pin baste and test the fit on the machine. Modify the sizes of the pieces to compensate for the bulk that will result from thick seam allowance and quilting.

Construction

1 ▪ Cut central panel and two ends from outer fabric, lining, and fleece, adding approximately 1 inch (2.5 cm) around all edges. The pieces will be trimmed to size after quilting.

2 ▪ Cut bias strips for a finished binding approximately ½ inch (1.5 cm) wide. Cut enough length to bind seams and the lower edge. Complete instructions for making and applying bias binding are on page 12.

3 ▪ Fuse fleece to the wrong side of the outer fabric sections.

4 ▪ Place wrong side of each lining section against the fleece and pin at close intervals.

5 ▪ Quilt the layers together according to the design of your choice. Trim to the pattern.

6 ▪ With right sides together, stitch end sections to the central panel.

7 ▪ Press the bias strips as described on page 12. Stitch the bindings to encase the seam allowances. Bind the lower edge.

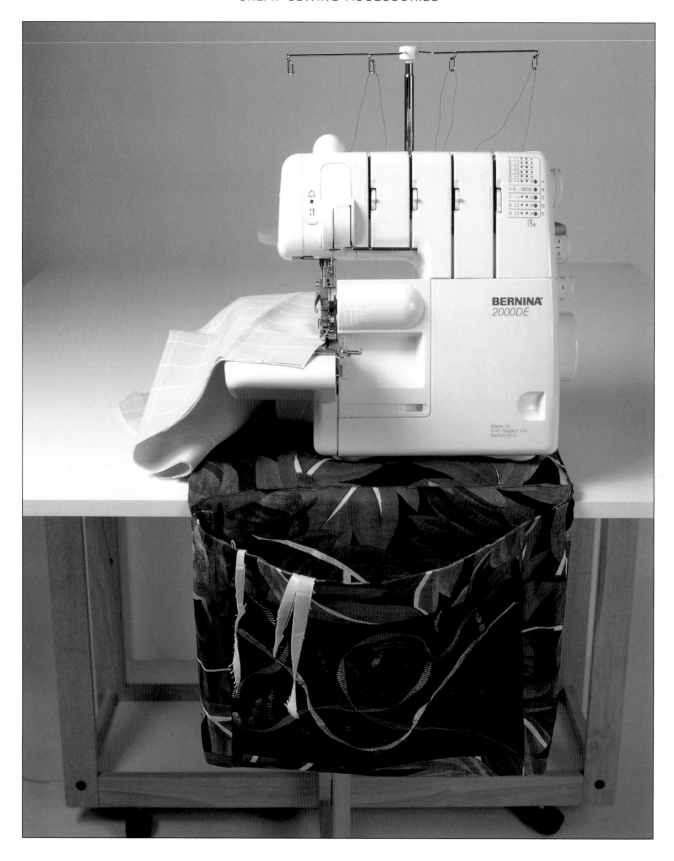

SEVERAL KINDS OF EFFICIENCY CAN BE COMBINED IN A SINGLE USEFUL ACCESSORY. *A foam pad under the serger makes for quiet sewing and reduces vibrations. And when the scrap-catcher is full, just hold it over the trash can and unzip the bottom.*

Zip-Clean Serger Silencer

designer: **Mary Parker**

The front of the scrap-catcher features a decorative panel to embellish with appliqué, machine embroidery, an original fabric painting—anything you like. The design in the photo features machine embroidery, with rayon and metallic thread, to repeat the pattern in the fabric.

The silencer pad is 15 inches (38 cm) square. The scrap-catcher is 15 inches (38 cm) wide, 12 inches (30 cm) long, and 3 inches (7.5 cm) deep. For fabric, choose a firm, medium-weight cotton or cotton blend.

Materials

- Fabric, 1¼ yards (1.15 m) 45 inches (115 cm) wide, or 1 yard (1 m) 54 or 60 inches (137 or 152 cm) wide
- Fabric for decorative panel, 12 by 9 inches (30.5 by 23 cm)
- Backing for decorative panel
- Foam, 1 inch (2.5 cm) thick, 14-inch (35-cm) square
- Lightweight fusible interfacing, 4 by 36 inch (10 by 91 cm) piece
- Zipper, 14 inches (35 cm)

Cutting

1 ▪ For the back and under cushion, cut one piece 28 inches (71 cm) long and 16 inches (40 cm) wide.

2 ▪ For the upper cushion, cut one piece 20 inches (51 cm) long and 16 inches (40 cm) wide. Mark a point 4½ inches (11 cm) up from the lower edge on each side seamline.

3 ▪ For the lower front, cut one piece 17 inches (43 cm) long and 16 inches (40 cm) wide.

4 ▪ Cut two sides, 17 inches (43 cm) long and 4 inches (10 cm) wide. Mark a point 4½ inches (11 cm) down from the top on one (the back) side seamline of each piece.

5 ▪ For the bottom, cut two pieces, 16 inches (40 cm) long and 2½ inches (7 cm) wide.

Construction

Allow ½ inch (1 cm) for all seams and hems. Sew seams with right sides together unless instructed otherwise.

1 ▪ Fuse a 15-inch (38-cm) strip of interfacing below the marked points on the wrong side of the cushion top section, keeping it free of the seam allowances. Clean finish the long edge.

2 ▪ Stitch the cushion top section to the back, aligning at top and sides, and ending the stitching at the marked points on the top section.

3 ▪ Fuse backing, if needed, to the decorative panel. Embellish it as you wish. Turn under the outer edges ½ inch (1 cm), mitering the corners neatly, and press.

4 ▪ Position the panel on the right side of the lower front section, 2½ inches (6 cm) up from the lower edge and centered between the sides. Stitch it in place with a decorative stitch or straight stitching close to the edges.

5 ▪ Install the zipper in the bottom section. Place the bottom sections with long together and stitch 1 inch (2.5 cm) at each end and baste the remainder of the seam. Center the zipper, face down, over the basted section of the seam and stitch along both sides. Remove the basting.

6 ▪ Stitch the bottom section to the unmarked ends of the side pieces.

7 ▪ Stitch the front to the bottom/side pieces, matching corners. Press seam allowances toward the sides.

8 ▪ Fuse the remaining interfacing strip section across the upper edge of the front/side section, placing it ½ inch (1 cm) from the top and between the side seam allowances. Clean finish the upper edge.

9 ▪ Pin the back to the front below marks at the sides, and across the lower edges. Pin the interfaced area of the upper cushion to the upper sides, clipping the seam allowance as necessary. Stitch.

10 ▪ Insert the cushion. Stitch cushion top to the back along the interfacing line.

11 ▪ Turn under and stitch the hem around the facing edge. Turn to the inside. If desired, topstitch around the upper edge of the opening.

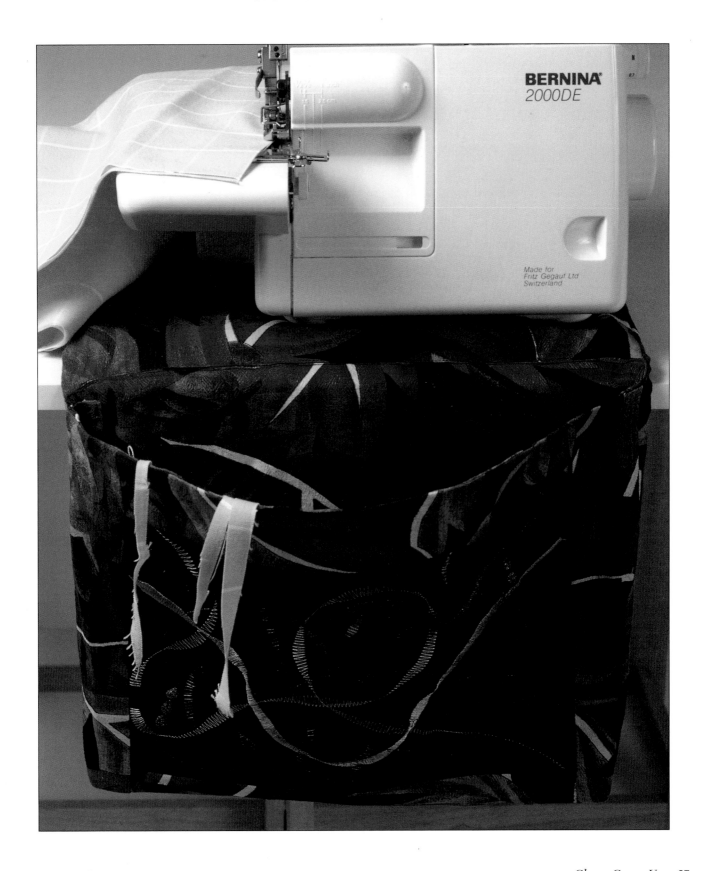

A SEWING MACHINE COVER PROVIDES A WONDERFUL BACKGROUND FOR EXPERIMENTAL STITCHING. *Practice a new technique with specialty threads. Play with some of your seldom-used machine accessories. Test the latest gadgets from the notions catalog. Once the pattern is made, the cover is quick to assemble and you can decorate to your heart's content.*

Appliquéd Machine Cover

The fabric blocks appliquéd onto this cover were not backed or neatly finished, but were simply stitched in place with assorted thread colors. For the fine lines, narrow strips of fabric were twisted and couched onto the cover with a zigzag stitch.

The cover was made to fit a machine with an irregularly shaped top, and with the snap-on sewing table in place. There are separate pieces for the top, front, back, and for each end. The top has a layer of batting between the outer fabric and lining to help it hold its shape. The layers are held together by the appliqué stitching. A cutout on top allows the cover to be put on with spools of thread on the spindles. The seam at one back corner was left open to accommodate the cords. The cover is assembled wrong side out, the seams covered with bias binding.

Materials

- Quantities will depend upon your pattern and design.
- Gridded pattern drafting material
- Fabric, in assorted colors, for cover sections, appliqué, and bias binding
- Very lightweight fusible interfacing for cover sections
- Fusible batting, for the top

Making the Pattern

1 ▪ Measure the machine sections and draft a pattern piece for the front, the back, each end if they are different, and the top. For the top, outline the opening for spools. Add ¼ inch (1 cm) seam allowance at all edges, but do not add hem allowance.

2 ▪ Cut out the pattern pieces, pin them together, and check the fit on the machine. Adjust if necessary.

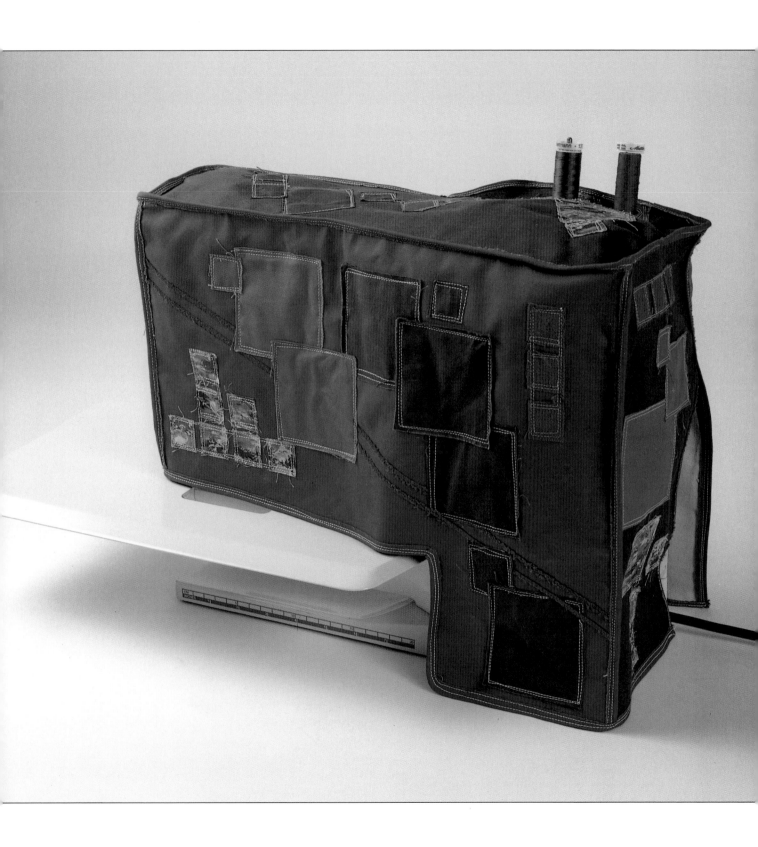

Construction

1 • Cut back, front, and end sections from fabric and from interfacing. Cut two top pieces from fabric and one from batting.

2 • Cut bias strips to make up enough length to bind both edges of the back opening, all seams, and the cover lower edge. For detailed instructions on making and applying bias, see page 12.

3 • Fuse interfacing to the wrong side of fabric sections. Fuse batting to outer top section. On the right side of this piece, mark the spool opening. Position lining against the batting and baste.

4 • Embellish the pieces with appliqué or as you wish, keeping the design areas within the seamlines.

5 • On the top, stitch around the marked opening with short stitches. Cut out the opening, cutting close to the stitching. Set the machine for a zigzag stitch at medium width and a length just slightly longer than for satin stitch. Stitch around the opening, overcasting the edge.

6 • Press folds in bias strips and bind the edges involved in the back opening.

7 • With wrong sides together, join front, ends and back. Leave the upper ¼ inch (1 cm) of each seam open. Overlap the seam allowances of the bound opening edges and baste across the upper seamline.

8 • Pin and stitch the top to the main section with wrong sides together.

9 • Stitch bias binding over each vertical seam. Bind the seam around the top, and bind the lower edge.

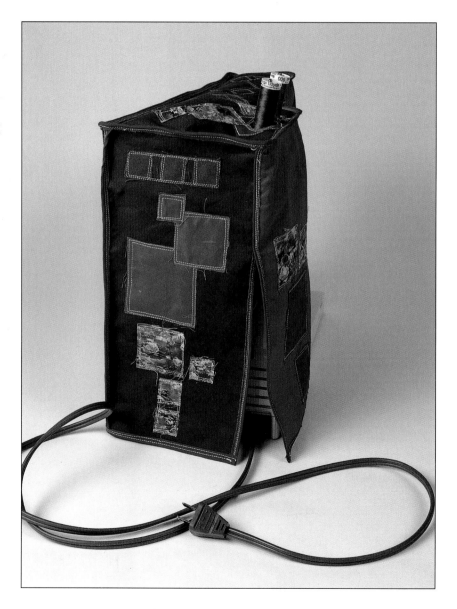

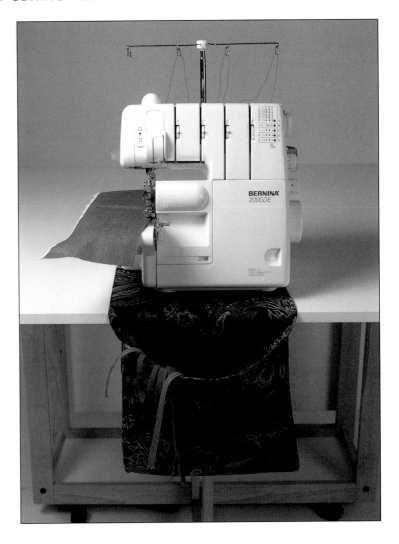

The Scrap-Catcher That Stays Open

designer: **Lori Kerr**

AN ENCASED WIRE KEEPS THE TOP OPEN TO ENSURE THAT SERGER TRIMMINGS LAND WHERE THEY ARE SUPPOSED TO. *Sewn into the upper section is a foam pad that helps keep the serger in place and reduces the noise level.*

Interior fabrics—chintz and other cottons intended for home decorating—work well for this and for other sewing room accessories. They are finished to resist soil and stains, and tend to retain their shape.

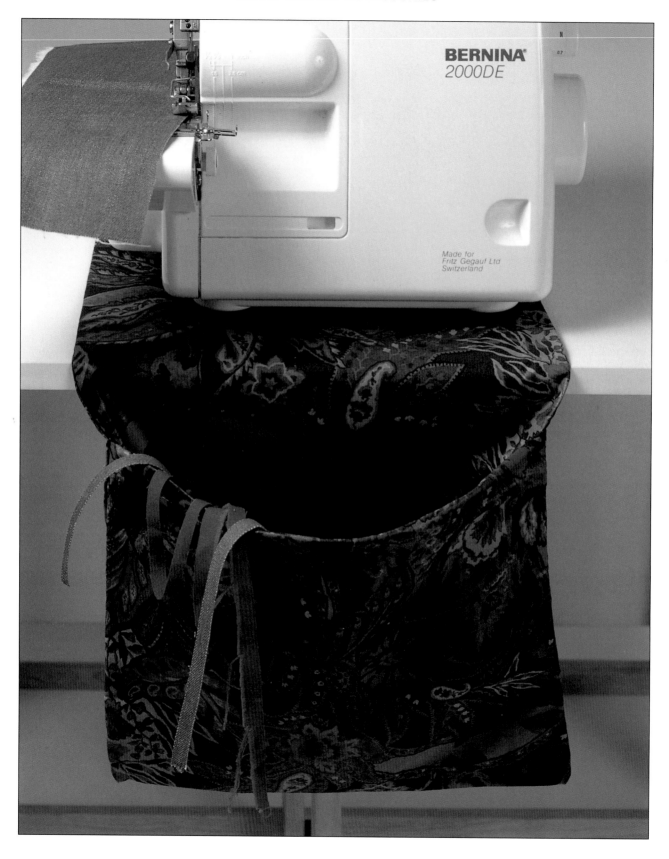

Materials

- Fabric, ¾ yard (.7 m)
- Wire hanger
- Foam pad, 1 inch (2.5 cm) thick, 10½ by 11 inches (26.5 by 28 cm)

Cutting

1 ▪ Cut one piece 22½ inches (57 cm) long and 12½ inches (31.5 cm) wide.

2 ▪ Cut one piece 34 inches (86.5 cm) long and 12½ inches (31.5 cm) wide.

3 ▪ Cut a piece 11¼ inches (28.5 cm) wide from the hanger.

Construction

All seam allowances are ⅝ inch (1.5 cm).

1 ▪ Hem one short end of each piece with a ½ inch (1.3 cm) double hem.

2 ▪ On the longer piece, turn the finished end 10 inches (25.5 cm) to the right side. Pin along the sides, but cheat on the seam allowance of the hemmed section toward the hemmed end. This will aid in keeping the top of the bag open.

3 ▪ Stitch one side. Insert the wire in the hem, then stitch that side, taking care to avoid the wire.

4 ▪ Pin this section to the other, right sides together, the fold even with the hemmed edge of the shorter section. Stitch, avoiding the wire ends. Turn right side out.

5 ▪ Press under the seam allowances at the open end. Insert the foam pad and edgestitch the opening.

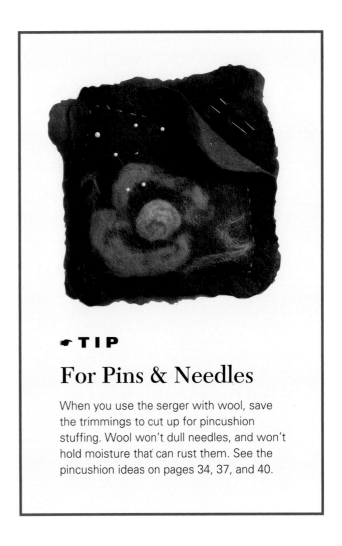

☛ TIP

For Pins & Needles

When you use the serger with wool, save the trimmings to cut up for pincushion stuffing. Wool won't dull needles, and won't hold moisture that can rust them. See the pincushion ideas on pages 34, 37, and 40.

IT'S GOOD-BYE TO SEWING TABLE CLUTTER!
An astounding number of small sewing essentials can be kept in order—and in sight—in one compact and colorful organizer. Marking pens and pencils, rulers and chalk, rippers and rolls of tape will be right where you can find them when you need them.

Spool
Caddy

designer: **Mary Parker**

With all the cords, trims, ribbons, and braids available, there is no limit to the decorating possibilities for the caddy. Here is a quick and inexpensive way to get organized, have some fun, and finally put your empty spool collection to good use.

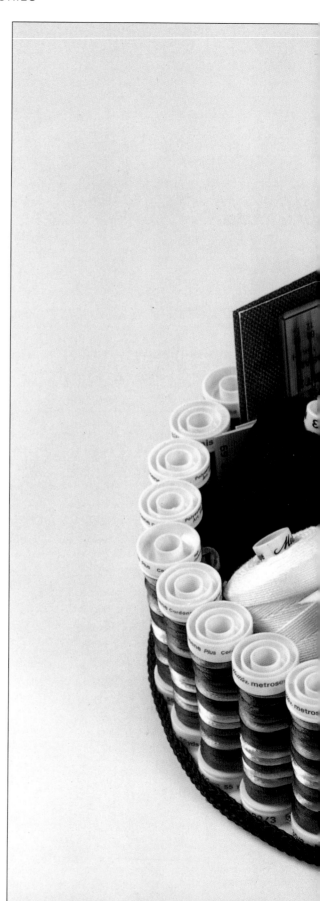

5
New Life for Old Treasure

Much of what you need to make your sewing room more efficient can be found in the basement, or perhaps in those boxes in the attic filled with saved and salvaged goodies. Empty thread spools (even the plastic ones!), fabric tubes and boards, and leftover PVC pipe are just a few of the interesting items that will be converted to useful, attractive sewing room aids on the following pages. We sewers perhaps should not be encouraged in our hoarding habits, but we all know that someday, somehow, there will be a use for everything that we don't throw away.

Materials

- Empty thread spools as shown in the photo, 33 small and 4 large
- Rayon cord, assorted colors, several yards (meters) each
- Foamcore, one piece 8½ inches (21.5 cm) in diameter
- Ribbon or decorative braid ¼ inch (.7 cm) wide, ⅞ yard (.8 m)
- White glue or epoxy

Construction

1 ▪ Arrange the small spools around the perimeter of the foamcore circle and glue them in place.

2 ▪ Decorate the spools with the colored cord. Start at the inside and thread a length of cord in and out between the spools. Go around twice to cover all the spools. Change colors as you wish, or use one color throughout.

3 ▪ Glue the four large spools in place. Using the photo as a guide, wrap and connect them with cord.

4 ▪ Glue braid around the edge of the foamcore circle.

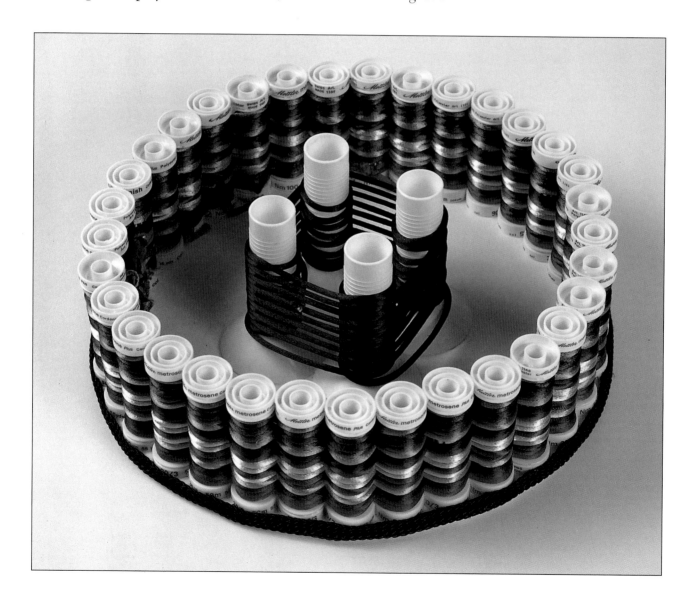

HANG FABRICS NEATLY TO KEEP THEM IN PRISTINE CONDITION. *Some fabrics, as you've probably discovered, develop permanent creases after they have been folded and stacked on a shelf for several years. This is an ideal way, too, to store fabrics that you have conscientiously preshrunk and pressed. They will be ready to sew when you are.*

Fine Fabric Holder

designer:
Dee Dee Triplett

The hanger is made with sturdy materials and can support as much fabric weight as your closet rod will tolerate. If your space permits, you may wish to use 23-inch (58-cm) lengths of PVC pipe so that you can store lengths of standard 45-inch (115-cm) fabrics folded just once. Increase the rope yardage accordingly.

Materials

- PVC pipe, ¾ inch (2 cm) diameter, 8 feet (2.45 m)
- Nylon rope, ⅜ inch (1 cm) diameter, 24 feet (7.35 m)
- Narrow ribbon or lightweight cord, 4 yards (3.7 m)

Construction

1 · Cut the pipe into six equal lengths.

2 · Fold the rope in half to determine the halfway point and mark a point 8 inches (20 cm) to either side.

3 · Thread one pipe section onto the center of the rope. Thread rope ends in opposite directions through another pipe, maintaining approximately 6 inches (15 cm) spacing between the pipes. Continue this way until all the pipe is in place.

4 · The pipes will tend to slip on the rope. To prevent this, tie the ropes together at each end of the pipe. Thread a bodkin or sturdy darning needle with a 12-inch (30-cm) length of ribbon or cord. Thread the ribbon between the strands of both rope sections at each end of each pipe. Tie the ends securely.

5 · Tie the rope ends over the closet rod with an overhand knot.

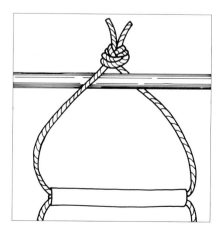

STORE PATTERNS AND FABRICS SMOOTHLY ON STURDY CARDBOARD TUBES. *Materials often arrive at fabric stores rolled onto these long tubes, and most stores would be pleased to know you have a use for the empty ones. They provide an efficient means of dealing with patterns that you don't want to fold, stiff interfacings, and fabrics that crease easily. Slipped into their custom holder, the tubes are within easy reach.*

Fabric Tube Holder

Our holder is 70 inches (177 cm) long and 32 inches (81 cm) wide. When the tubes are in place it contracts in length to approximately 48 to 56 inches (122 to 142 cm). The ties on this one slip over heavy-duty picture molding hooks for hanging. An alternative is to add stitching across the top for a casing and use a sturdy dowel or length of PVC pipe to hang it. Keep in mind that the filled holder will be quite heavy if it is used to store fabric.

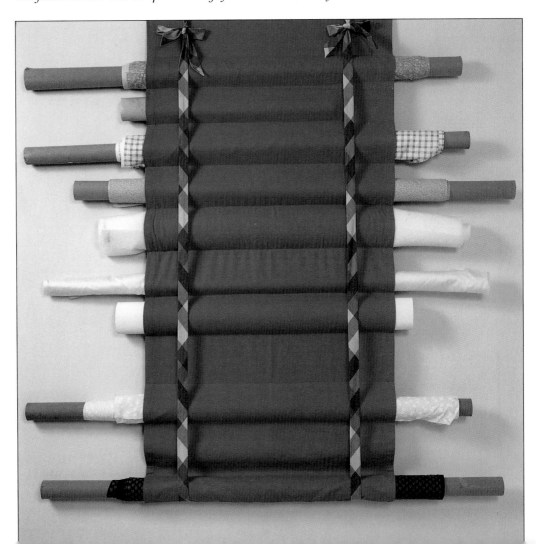

Materials

- Fabric for the holder (see step 1)

- Fabric for ties, 1 yard (.95 m), 45 inches (115 cm) wide. As an alternative, use 8 yards (7.35 m) of firmly woven braid, twill tape, or other decorative trim 1½ to 2 inches (4 to 5 cm) wide. The tie material should not stretch.

- Cardboard tubes

Construction

1 ▪ Determine fabric yardage required; you will need one piece, 36 inches (91 cm) wide and 4 yards (3.7 m) long. For fabric 36 or 45 inches (90 or 115 cm) wide, you will need 4 yards (3.7 m); for 54-inch (137-cm) fabric, 3 yards (2.75 m). For fabric this width it will be necessary to piece the back. With 60-inch (152-cm) fabric, it is more economical to make a holder that finishes 26 inches (66 cm) wide. If the chosen fabric is costly, consider using sturdy cotton drill for the back.

2 ▪ Stitch the ends of the fabric together to form a large tube.

3 ▪ Hem both sides of the fabric with 1-inch (2.5-cm) double hems.

4 ▪ Position the fabric with the seam at the top and stitch across the doubled fabric approximately 1 inch (2.5 cm) from the top.

5 ▪ Mark and pin stitching lines across the fabric, placing them 6 to 8 inches (15 to 20 cm) apart or as needed to accommodate the tubes you will use. Stitch, backstitching securely at the ends of the seams.

6 ▪ For the ties, cut fabric strips 4 inches (10 cm) wide on the lengthwise fabric grain (so they will not stretch). Join ends to make two long strips.

7 ▪ Press under the seam allowances on the long edges of the strips. Angle the ends. Fold each strip in half right side out and press. Stitch close to both sides and across the ends.

8 ▪ Insert the tubes in the holder, then loop the ties around it and tie them securely for hanging.

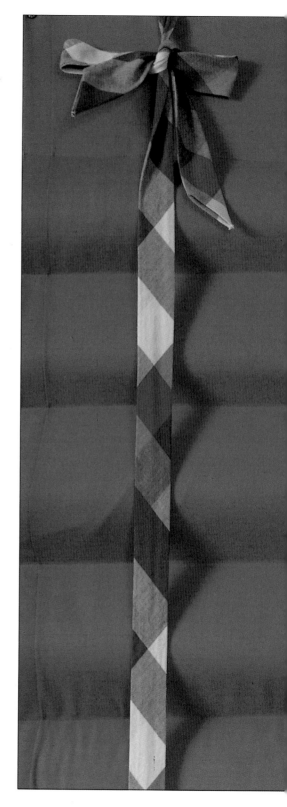

SHARE YOUR TREASURED COLLECTION OF WOODEN SPOOLS. *With this elegant table you can display the collection where others can enjoy and appreciate it too.*

Spool Table designer: **Pat Scheible**

The table shown is 10 by 19 inches (25 by 48 cm) and stands 20 inches (50.5 cm) high. Spools used for the legs are approximately 2⅜ inches (6 cm) high. Smaller spools, such as those used for silk button-hole twist, could be used to make a scaled-down variation of the design—a charming curio shelf or miniature étagère.

Materials and Tools

- 32 large wooden spools
- 2 pieces of ¼ inch (.7 cm) plywood, 10 by 19 inches (25 by 48 m)
- 4 dowels, ³⁄₁₆ inch (.5 cm) diameter, approximately 20 inches (20.5 cm) long
- 4 small wood screws
- Drill, with small bit, ³⁄₁₆-inch (.5-cm) bit, and countersink bit
- Carpenter's glue or epoxy
- Wood filler
- Paint, for the table: primer, and flat latex or acrylic in the desired color
- Paint for stencils: latex or acrylic craft paint
- Permanent marking pen, for decorative lines
- Stencil medium such as stencil board or mylar
- Natural sponge, for stencils
- Decorative cord or heavy thread to wrap the spools
- Double-sided tape

Construction

1 ▪ Use one of the spools as a guide for marking placement points for legs on both pieces of plywood.

2 ▪ Bore holes through one piece of plywood (the shelf) to accommodate the dowels.

3 ▪ Drill a pilot hole at the center of one end (the upper end) of each dowel.

4 ▪ Assemble the table without gluing to check the length of the dowels. Trim them even with the top of the uppermost spool. Adjust if necessary.

5 ▪ For each leg, thread three spools onto a dowel, using a drop or so of glue to secure each one. Put the shelf in place. Add five spools.

6 ▪ Drill a countersink hole at each marked point on the top. Glue the top in place and screw it to the dowels. Fill the holes.

Painting and Decorating

1 ▪ Prime all sides of the top and shelf. Sand lightly, and add one or two finish coats.

2 ▪ Cut stencils in the desired designs.

3 ▪ Pour a small puddle of paint for the stenciling. Dab a small piece of natural sponge into the paint, and dab it onto newspapers until it is almost dry. Work the stencil from the outer edges inward.

4 ▪ Add accents and design lines with the marking pen.

5 ▪ For the legs, wrap each spool with double-sided tape. Wrap thread or cord neatly, applying a drop of glue to each end.

6 ▪ To protect the artwork, use clear acrylic when the paint is thoroughly dry. Alternatively, have a piece of glass cut to fit.

ENLARGE PATTERNS 145%

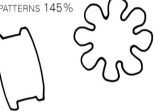

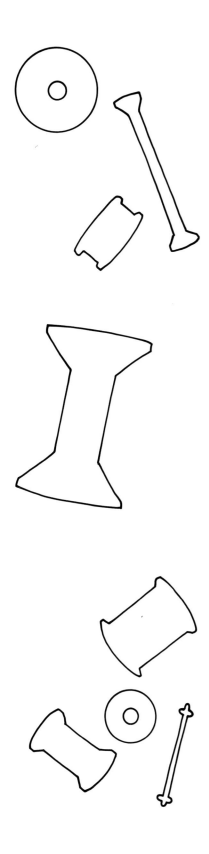

Speaking of Recycling…

There are alternatives to the ubiquitous plastic pattern weights. Patternmaker Tracy Doyle saves 35 mm film canisters and fills them with sand for use in the sewing room.

Designer Pat Scheible uses any small, heavy, interesting object she can find (with emphasis on the latter). Her collection includes antique iron gear wheels, smooth stones gathered in far-away places, a Sumi ink bottle filled with sand, and an old flatiron.

MOST FABRIC STORES ARE DELIGHTED TO GIVE AWAY THE EMPTY BOARDS FROM BOLTS OF FABRIC. *They are sturdy, and hollow, and a few of them taped together make a very serviceable bulletin board.*

The boards come in different lengths. The longer ones, used for fabric 60 to 64 inches (152 to 162 cm) wide, make a more generously sized bulletin board. We used three for the board shown. On the back, use glue-on picture hangers or tape picture wire in place.

Instant Bulletin Board

Materials

- Fabric boards, two to four of the same length
- Fabric, enough to cover boards with ample margin
- Fiberfill batting, slightly smaller than fabric
- Hooks for hanging the board
- Duct tape
- Piece of foamcore or stiff cardboard as long as the combined board width

Optional:

- Trim to edge the board perimeter
- Fabric glue or decorative tacks

Construction

1 ▪ Place the boards side by side and upside down on a flat surface. Tape them tightly together, placing a strip near each end. Wrap tape just around the edges, not across the front—it's difficult to get a pin through it.

2 ▪ Tape the length of foamcore across the back of the boards at about the center.

3 ▪ Place the board face down on the batting and wrap it tightly around all edges. Clip away excess at the corners to reduce bulk. Tape it firmly.

4 ▪ Attach the fabric in the same way, but miter the corners neatly.

5 ▪ Attach trim around the edge of the board, if desired.

PROTECT YOUR GOOD SHEARS AND KEEP THEM HANDY AT THE SAME TIME IN A CUSTOM-FITTED HOLDER. *Hang it on the sewing chair or in another convenient place while you work. Then roll it up, shears and all, when you've finished and hide it away from the kids and husband for safekeeping.*

Scissors Holster

The case is made of medium-weight synthetic suede for durability. The back section is double thickness; the upper layer is hemmed at an angle and eased to fit over the blades. It accommodates a pair each of 9-inch (23-cm) shears, 8-inch (20-cm) shears, and 7-inch (18-cm) pinking shears.

Materials

- Synthetic suede, two pieces 5¼ inches by 14¼ inches (13 by 36 cm) and one piece slightly larger. You will also need two strips, 12 inches (30 cm) long and 1 inch (2.5 cm) wide.

- Fusible web or fabric glue

Construction

1 ▪ For the back section, glue baste or lightly fuse the two rectangles together, right sides out (they will be stitched later). Leave an open spot at each upper corner to insert the ties.

2 ▪ Arrange the shears on the back, angled as shown in the photo. With chalk, mark the upper ends of the blades. Place the remaining fabric piece over the shears, right side up. Fold under along the angled edge at the marked points, leaving some excess at the other side and lower edge. Press the fold and topstitch along it with two rows of stitching.

3 ▪ Ease the upper section to fit over the shears. The fit should be snug enough to keep the shears in place, but not so tight that it's difficult to put them

in place. Position one pair at a time, beginning at the bottom. Chalk mark around the blades on the upper fabric, and glue baste along the marks. Sew a double row of stitching along the marked lines.

4 ▪ Glue baste the sections together around the edges.

5 ▪ Make the ties. Fold each tie section in half right side out. Glue baste, and stitch close to both edges. Slip the ends of the ties between the back fabric layers at the upper corners. Glue baste them in place.

6 ▪ Topstitch the sections together around the edges, stitching close to the edge and again approximately ¼ inch (.5 cm) in.

6
A Place for Everything

For yourself or for gifts, here is a selection of innovative accessories to help keep your sewing life in order, and add a decorative touch to the sewing room at the same time. When tools where you need them and materials where you can find them, it's a pleasure to begin a new project.

DON'T YOU WISH YOU COULD EASILY KEEP TRACK OF ALL YOUR GREAT DESIGN IDEAS AND SEWING DISCOVERIES?

A special notebook just for the purpose is a great way to start. If you make a pair of them while you're at it, you will have a wonderful gift ready to give a sewing friend.

The Sewer's Journal

designer:
Dee Dee Triplett

As for the contents, we've shown several possibilities. Make fabric pages—edge them in contrasting fabric if you wish—for a visual record of your machines stitches, both decorative and utility. Photos in the manual never quite get the point across. Try experimenting with stitch width and length settings, too. You will have a ready reference for some future project without wasting time and fabric to accomplish what you want to do.

Include samples of different threads. There are so many new ones to play with.

Include the disasters, too. It's just as important to know what not to do in the future.

For the ultimate in organization, keep a record of the fabric you have stashed away. Make up a sheet like the one shown, or with whatever information you would like to have, and make photocopies for your notebook.

Materials

- Three-ring binder, approximately 10 by 12 inches (25.5 by 30.5 cm)
- Fabric for the cover, ¾ yard (.7 m) at 45 inches (115 cm) wide
- Fleece or thin batting, ¾ yard (.7 m)
- For the hands, sueded fabric 8 by 10 inches (20 by 25.5 cm)
- Paper-backed fusible web, 8 by 10 inches (20 by 25.5 cm)
- Contrast fabric, 9 by 12 inches (23 by 30.5 cm), for the inner pocket and spool appliqué
- Second contrast fabric for the pocket edging and thread on the appliquéd spool
- Silver lame fabric, a small scrap for the needle appliqué
- Metallic thread for the cover design
- Invisible thread for the appliqué

Instructions

1 ▪ Check that your binder will bend open in the backward direction far enough that the covers can be slipped into the flaps on the fabric cover. If not, make the inner flaps narrower.

2 ▪ Place the main cover fabric right side down. Layer the batting on top. To find the position for the front cover appliqué, place the binder atop the batting in the center of the 45-inch (115-cm) side, 1 inch (2.5 cm) up from the edge. It may be helpful to align the center of the binder spine with the center crease in the fabric. Mark placement of the front cover and inner pocket with pins or chalk.

3 ▪ Prepare the appliqué pieces. Trace and enlarge the designs. Trace the patterns onto the paper side of the fusible web. Fuse them to the wrong side of the appropriate fabric pieces. Cut the pieces and pin them in place on the cover.

4 ▪ Make the pocket. Cut the pocket fabric 9 by 7 inches (23 by 18 cm). Cut trim 2 by 9 inches (5 by 23 cm). Stitch the 9-inch (23-cm) sides of the two pieces together, using ½ inch (1 cm) seam allowance. Press all edges ½ inch (1.5 cm) to the wrong side. Pin inside the front cover. Recheck positioning of the pocket and appliqué pieces with the cover on the binder.

5 ▪ Sew the pocket to the cover. Fuse the appliqué pieces and blindstitch the edges with invisible thread. Stitch the finger divisions by machine with thread to match the fabric. Use metallic thread to stitch the needle thread on the cover design.

6 ▪ Pin the 45-inch (115-cm) edges of the cover together to form a long tube. Slip onto the binder to adjust the fit, allowing for the thickness of the fleece when the cover is turned right side out. Stitch. Turn right side out.

7 ▪ Turn under the edges at the open ends ½ inch (1.5 cm). Press, and stitch. Slip the binder in place.

ENLARGE PATTERN 150%

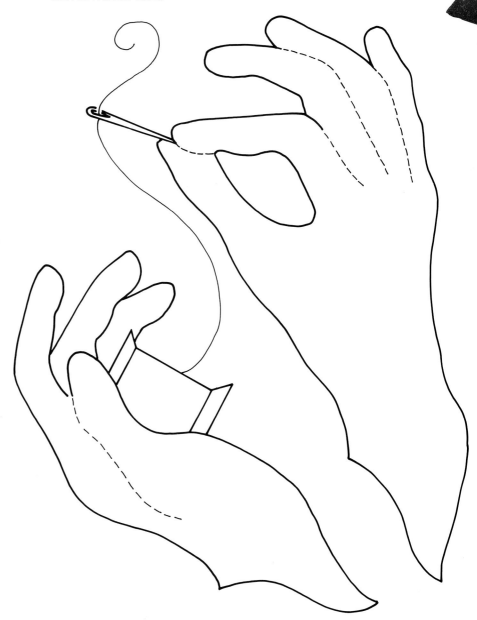

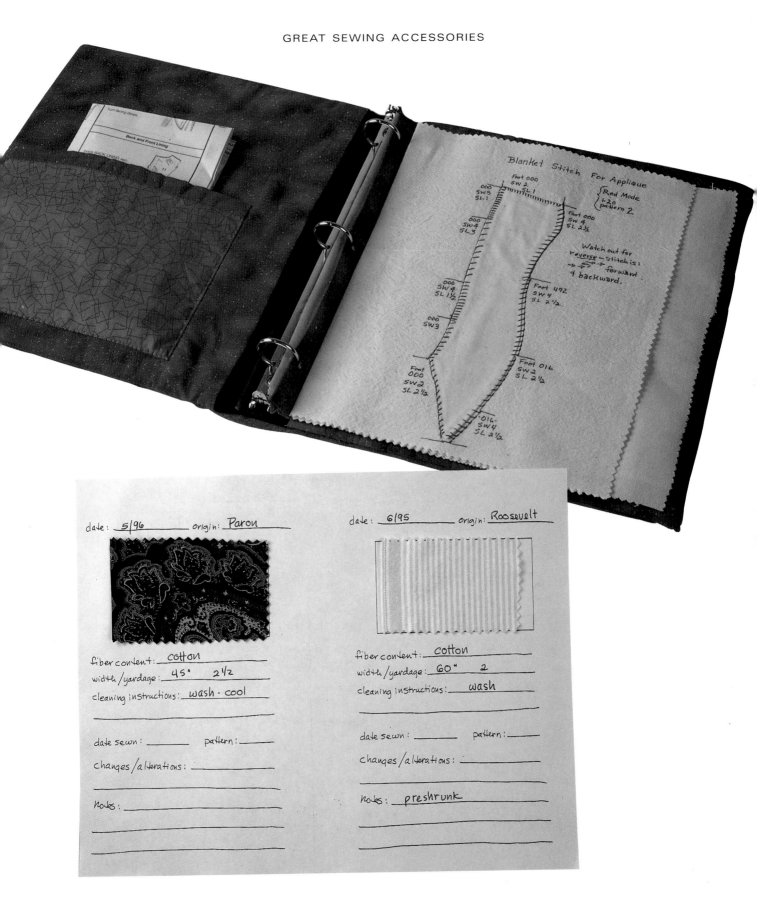

Blanket Stitch For Applique

Foot 000
SW 2
SL 1

000
SW3
SL 1

Red Mode
t 20
pattern 2

000
SW4
SL 3

Foot 000
SW 4
SL 2½

Watch out for
reverse — stitch is:
→ ⇒ forward
⇐ backward.

000
SW 4
SL 1½

Foot 492
SW 4
SL 2½

000
SW 3

Foot 016
SW 2
SL 2½

Foot
000
SW 2
SL 2½

016
SW 4
SL 2½

date: 5/96   origin: Paron

fiber content: cotton
width/yardage: 45"   2½
cleaning instructions: wash · cool

date sewn: _____   pattern: _____

changes/alterations: _____

notes: _____

date: 6/95   origin: Roosevelt

fiber content: cotton
width/yardage: 60"   2
cleaning instructions: wash

date sewn: _____   pattern: _____

changes/alterations: _____

notes: preshrunk

RESULTS OF AN UNOFFICIAL SURVEY INDICATE THAT SEWERS WHO ARE FORTUNATE ENOUGH TO HAVE THEIR OWN WORK SPACE NEVER EVER PUT AWAY AN IRONING BOARD. *The bulky pressing equipment can occupy a great deal of shelf space that might otherwise be used to store more fabric, so why not make a storage area of the wasted space under the ironing board?*

Pressing Organization

designer: **Mary Parker**

This clever equipment caddy consists of two lengths of heavy cotton drill (canvas would work as well), held together around the ironing board legs with hook and loop tape. Lengths of PVC pipe or wooden dowel slip into casings at the upper and lower edges of each section to stabilize the pieces and support the weight. Ties are sewn along the upper edge of each piece, pulled up through the holes in the ironing board, and tied tightly together.

Both back and front sections of this caddy are 38 inches (96 cm) wide and 33 inches (84 cm) wide. Ironing boards vary considerably, so read through the instructions and diagram your own measurements to determine fabric requirements.

While you're at it, make a new ironing board cover to match. This one is made of the same fabric as the caddy and is embroidered with a very useful 1-inch (2.5 cm) grid.

Materials

- Fabric, heavy cotton drill or canvas, the same amount for both the front and back sections, and additional yardage for pockets
- Fabric for the ironing board cover (see instructions)
- Cotton batting, for the ironing board cover, enough for a double layer
- Elastic, for the perimeter of the ironing board cover
- Thread and backing material for embroidery, if desired
- PVC pipe or wooden dowel, approximately ½ to ⅝ inch (1.5 cm) diameter, four pieces cut to the finished caddy width
- Twill tape, ½ inch (1.3 cm) wide, 3 yards (2.75 m)
- Hook and loop tape, approximately 30 inches (76 cm)

Calculating Fabric Requirements

1 ▪ Cotton drill fabric and some canvas will shrink considerably. If you intend to launder the caddy some day, wash and machine dry the fabric before cutting to preshrink it. Do this twice just to be safe.

2 ▪ Determine finished measurements for the caddy front and back. Allow for 1¼-inch (3-cm) double hems at the sides. At top and bottom of each, allow for stitching ½ inch (1 cm) above/below the edge of the piece, then allow for the casing and hem.

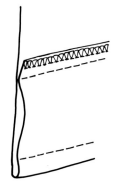

3 ▪ Refer to the pocket instructions that follow. Determine the style, size and number of pockets, then figure your fabric needs.

Construction: CADDY

1 ▪ Hem both sides of each caddy section with a double hem.

2 ▪ Clean finish the upper and lower edges of both pieces. On each upper and lower edge, fold to the wrong side for the hem and rod casing as shown above. Stitch across the piece ½ inch (1 cm) below/above the fold, then again to form the casing.

3 ▪ Cut twill tape into twelve lengths. At the top of one section, mark positions for the ties. Place one at each side hem and space the other four evenly across. Fold under an end of each and stitch with an X in the margin above the rod casing on the wrong side of the piece. Stitch ties opposite these on the other section.

4 ▪ Cut the hook and loop tape into pieces approximately 2 inches (5 cm) long and stitch them at intervals along the side hems. If you wish, complete this step after sewing on the pockets.

Construction: POCKETS AND HOLDERS

Three different kinds of pockets and holders are used on the model. We placed pockets only on the front section, but more can be added on the back if your space allows. Plan for some of the heavier items to be stored on each side to balance the weight.

The pockets provide plenty of opportunity for embellishment in the form of appliqué, embroidery, or whatever you wish. Think of the piece as a big, blank canvas, just waiting for your creative touch.

PATCH POCKETS

For items that aren't too bulky, such as rulers, these work well.

1 ▪ Cut fabric twice the desired finished length with seam allowance added at all edges.

2 ▪ Fold the pocket in half, wrong side out, across the width.

3 ▪ Stitch each pocket, leaving an opening in the side opposite the fold for turning. Trim the corners, turn, and press. Press under the seam allowances along the openings.

4 ▪ Topstitch in place along the sides and lower edges, reinforcing at the upper corners. If desired, stitch vertical lines to subdivide the pocket.

BOX POCKETS

These accommodate very bulky items like the pressing ham. They are interesting to make.

1 ▪ Place fabric over the item to determine the size and placement. Mark the placement lines for sides and lower edge on the caddy section.

2 ▪ To determine cutting length for the pocket, figure the desired height and add the necessary depth (front to back). To this, add a hem allowance at the top and seam allowance at the bottom.

3 ▪ For the cutting width, determine the finished width and add seam allowance at both sides.

4 ▪ Hem the upper edge. Clean finish the sides and lower edge.

5 ▪ Turn under and press the side seam allowances. Using the placement lines on the caddy as a guide, fold a square corner at the bottom of the pocket on each side as shown. Baste the pleats in place along the back seamline.

6 ▪ With right sides together, stitch the pocket to the caddy.

7 ▪ On the right side, crease the pocket from front to back at the side/bottom corner. Stitch close to the crease.

HOLDERS

These work well for items that are shaped for hanging, such as scissors or a tape measure.

1 ▪ Figure the needed width of the piece and add seam allowance at each end. For the length (height), double the desired finished height and add seam allowance at both edges. Cut fabric this size.

2 ▪ Fold the piece in half the long way, right sides together, and stitch along the long edges. Turn right side out and clean finish the ends.

3 ▪ Stitch the piece to the backing, using the tool as a guide for placement. Stitch with right sides together if possible, otherwise turn under the seam allowances and topstitch in place.

Construction: IRONING BOARD COVER

2 ▪ Place the board upside down on the fabric piece and mark the outline. Add 4 inches (10 cm) or more for the board width, the hem, and elastic casing. Cut the fabric.

2 ▪ Cut two layers of batting so they extend just slightly over the edges of the board.

3 ▪ Stitch the double hem/casing around the cover, leaving an opening at the flat end.

4 ▪ With the cover on the board, thread the elastic through the casing and adjust it to fit tightly. Stitch the ends of the elastic securely, and stitch across the opening.

THIS MAGNIFICENT WALL HANGING IS FIRST OF ALL A WORK OF ART. *Its usefulness is simply a nice bonus. Assorted styles of pockets and holders keep sewing tools in perfect order.*

A Practical Tapestry

designer: **Lori Kerr**

A wall organizer offers a fine opportunity to employ a favorite technique or experiment with a new one. In this case, the background fabric is quilted with smoke-colored invisible thread using free motion straight stitching. The motifs were cut from a compatible fabric and appliquéd over top, matched across the pockets to unify the design.

The designer chose decorator fabrics, which offer a good range of design "families." These fabrics also are treated for soil and stain resistance, and sewing room lint can easily be brushed off them. Decorator cottons tend to be very stable, an advantage with a hanging of this size. Quilt batting is used between the layers for this model, but plain muslin could be substituted for the inner layer.

The instructions are for pockets of the specific sizes and shapes that the designer needed most. You may wish to alter some of them to accommodate your own tools. The finished organizer is approximately 31 inches (78.5 cm) wide and 40 inches (101.5 cm) long. It is hung by means of a lattice strip through a sleeve on the back.

Materials

- Fabric, 1¼ yards (1.15 m) for the top and pockets
- Fabric for appliqués, ½ to ¾ yard (.5 to .7 m)
- Muslin, for backing, 1¼ yard (1.15 m)
- Fabric for lining, sleeve, and edge binding, 1¾ yards (1.6 m)
- Fleece, batting, or muslin, 1 yard (.95 m)
- Scrap of semi-transparent fabric such as organza
- Fiberfill or other stuffing for pincushion
- Paper-backed fusible web for appliqué
- Threads: invisible thread for quilting, decorative threads for appliqué, and all-purpose thread for construction
- Wooden lattice strip, 31 inches (78.5 cm) long

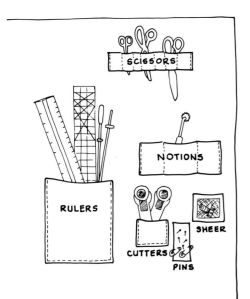

Cutting

1 ▪ Cut the top fabric, batting, and muslin backing 33 by 42 inches (84 by 106.5 cm)

2 ▪ Mark off a piece of the lining fabric 33 by 42 inches (84 by 106.5 cm); it will be cut to size later. From this fabric, cut a strip 33 inches by 10 inches (84 cm by 25 cm) for the sleeve in which the lattice strip will be inserted for hanging. Cut bias strips 3⅛ inches (8 cm) wide, enough to make up a single piece 150 inches (380 cm) long. Remember to allow for piecing seams.

3 ▪ Cut the pockets from the top fabric according to the dimensions given below, or according to your own size requirements. These measurements allow for the pockets to be folded double, then stitched and turned.

- Ruler pocket: 11½ by 28 inches (29 by 71 cm)
- Rotary cutter pocket: 6 by 12 inches (15 by 30.5 cm)
- See-through pocket: 5 by 10 inches (12.5 by 25.5 cm)
- Notions pocket: 13 by 12 inches (33 by 30.5 cm)
- Scissors holder: 28 by 3½ inches (71 by 8.5 cm)
- Pincushion: 3½ by 14 inches (8.5 cm by 35.5 cm)

Make the Pockets

All seam allowances are ⅝ inch (1.5 cm) except where instructed otherwise.

1 ▪ For the ruler, rotary cutter, see-through pockets, and the pincushion, fold the fabric in half crosswise, with right sides together. Pin.

2 ▪ Fold the notions pocket along the 12-inch (30.5-cm) side, and the scissors holder along the 28-inch (71-cm) side. Pin.

3 ▪ Stitch each pocket, leaving an opening in the side opposite the fold for turning. Trim the corners, turn, and press. Press under the seam allowances along the openings.

4 ▪ For the see-through pocket, cut a piece of organza or other fabric approximately ¾ inch (2 cm) smaller all around than the pocket. Center it on the pocket and zigzag it in place. Carefully cut the fabric from behind the organza, cutting close to the stitching. On the right side, go over the stitching with satin stitch.

5 ▪ Position the pockets on the top fabric using the photo or your design as a guide. Keep them at least 2 inches (5 cm) from the outer edges. It is helpful to put the tools in place while you do the arranging. Don't stitch the pockets yet.

Appliqué

1 ▪ Cut appliqué motifs and fuse the appliqué backing to them.

2 ▪ Arrange the motifs on the main fabric section. For interest, allow some of them to overlap the pockets, then cut these at the pocket edges. Fuse these pieces to the pocket sections. Fuse the motifs in place on the main section. Chalk mark the placement lines for the pockets and remove them.

3 ▪ Stitch the appliqué pieces to the pockets and the main section. Use several rows of straight stitch, and/or use one or more decorative threads. Try embroidery stitches for this step, too. Stitch around some of the design lines within the motifs to add texture.

Quilting

1 ▪ Sandwich the muslin, batting, and top fabric. Pin at intervals to keep the layers together.

2 ▪ Free motion stipple stitch was used to quilt this organizer, but you can use any design or pattern. With invisible thread, the texture shows, but the stitches do not. Fine smoke-colored nylon thread was used here because of the dark fabric colors.

3 ▪ Outline the appliqué motifs to add dimension.

4 ▪ Square up the piece and trim the edges evenly.

Attaching the Pockets

1 ▪ Replace the pockets in their marked positions, folded edges upward. For the scissors holder and notions pocket, put the tools in place so you can establish the needed amount of ease and mark the lines at which to stitch the vertical divisions.

2 ▪ Topstitch the pockets in place along the sides and lower edges, reinforcing at the upper corners. Stitch vertical lines on the notions pocket. Stitch the scissors holder at the ends and along the lines marked for the vertical divisions.

3 ▪ For the pincushion, stitch in place across the top and along the sides. Stuff it firmly, then stitch across the lower edge.

Finishing

1 ▪ Cut the lining piece to the size of the organizer.

2 ▪ Stitch a double hem in each end of the sleeve fabric, making the finished width of the piece approximately 4 inches (10 cm) less than the width of the lining.

3 ▪ Fold the strip in half across the width. Center it on the lining right side, the upper raw edges aligned with the lining upper edge. Stitch across the top within the seam allowance. Stitch close to the folded edge.

4 ▪ Apply the bias binding around the edges. Detailed instructions are on page 13.

Upholstered Boxes

Upholstered Boxes

WITH BRIGHT FABRIC COVERS, HUMBLE CARDBOARD CARTONS ASSUME A DECORATIVE AIR. *Cardboard boxes seem almost indispensable in the sewing room for dealing with the accumulation of buttons, patterns, scraps, trims, threads, zippers, and all the miscellaneous bits and pieces that won't fit into drawers or shelves. Even so, the room need not have the ambience of a recycling center. The boxes are just as practical dressed up.*

The boxes we've shown are unadorned, all kinds of embellishments might be added. Trims and unusual buttons can be glued in place after the boxes are finished. You might also appliqué or embroider the fabric beforehand.

Sturdy boxes with lids, like those illustrated here, are available in crafts supply stores. Commercially made pattern boxes, too, are good candidates for covering. Most corrugated cartons are not strong enough to hold up well.

Choose a medium to fairly heavy fabric so glue won't seep through and to hide any irregularities on the surface of the box. visible. Check that fabric is not so heavy that it interferes with the fit of the lid at the corners where there will be several layers. Decorator cottons are a good choice; they are medium weight and are heavily finished to resist soil and stains. Add a layer of polyester batting around the outside and one or two layers on the lid top to soften the sharp angles and edges.

Spray adhesive is an easy means of attaching fabrics. As an alternative, use good white fabric glue. Spread a thin, even coat over a small area at a time with a piece of stiff cardboard.

A useful tool for this project is the bookbinder's bone folder, used to smooth glued fabric and to work fabric into corners. A bamboo or plastic point turner and creaser is the same shape and a good substitute. Use the tool only to work the fabric, not to spread glue.

Materials and Tools

Quantities will depend upon the size of the box to be covered.

- Fabric for the outer covering
- Fabric for lining
- Spray adhesive or white glue
- Polyester batting
- Pinking shears
- Bone folder or point turner

Cutting

Instructions pertain to the square box with a fitted lid.

1 ▪ Cut a fabric piece for the outside of the box, in length, the height of the box plus 2 inches (5 cm); in width, the outer circumference of the box plus ¾ inch (2 cm). Trim one side edge—the edge that will overlap—with pinking shears.

2 ▪ Cut a piece for the bottom of the box, ½ inch (1.5 cm) smaller all around than the box bottom dimensions.

3 ▪ For the lid, measure from the inner lid, ½ inch (1.5 cm) in from the edge, down and around the edge of the lid, over the top, down and around the opposite edge, to a point ½ inch (1.5 cm) in from the edge on the inner lid. Cut a fabric this size.

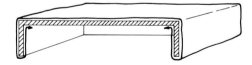

4 ▪ Cut a box lining piece, in length, the height of the box side; in width, the inner circumference of the box plus ¾ inch (2 cm). Pink the upper edge of the piece and down one side (the overlapping side).

5 ▪ Cut lining for the inner box bottom with pinking shears, ½ inch (1.5 cm) smaller all around than box bottom dimensions.

6 ▪ Cut the lid lining with pinking shears, ¼ inch (.5 cm) smaller all around than the inner lid dimensions.

7 ▪ Cut batting for the outer box, in width, the circumference of the box; in height, the height of the box side minus the lid depth.

8 ▪ Cut one or more layers of batting for the lid top. Cut the first to the lid dimensions, and cut each subsequent layer slightly smaller. When batting is glued to the lid, place the smallest layer next to the lid and largest layer on top.

Construction

1 ▪ Glue batting around the outer box, beginning at a corner and aligning the lower edge of the batting with the box lower edge.

2 ▪ Cover the outer box. Start at one corner with the straight fabric edge and glue fabric to the outer sides with a 1-inch (2.5 cm) margin top and bottom.

3 ▪ Glue lower margin to the box bottom, mitering the corners neatly.

4 ▪ Glue upper margin to the inside of the box, pressing fabric smoothly into corners.

5 ▪ Glue the outer and inner bottom pieces in place.

6 ▪ Glue batting layers to the top of the lid.

7 ▪ Spread glue to the outer sides of the lid, one at a time, to attach the fabric (the fabric can't be glued to the batting). Fold neatly at the corners, trimming away under layers of fabric to reduce bulk. Glue the opposite side next, pulling the fabric evenly taut across the batting. Glue the remaining sides in the same way.

8 ▪ Glue fabric to the inner edges of the lid, pressing fabric well into corners and smoothing fabric edges.

9 ▪ Glue the lid lining in place.

The Round box

Measure, cut and glue fabrics as for the square box; only the lid is handled differently. When gluing the fabric around the outer edge of the lid, smooth it into neat, regular pleats. Glue a strip of trim or gimp around the edge, if desired, or tie on a ribbon.

An Eclectic Room: Functional and Fun

designer: **Pat Scheible**

THE resident and designer of this enchanting room is a professional artist and an incorrigible collector of anything that speaks to her or that exhibits potential as an ingredient for some future work of art. The room itself is an exhibition, constantly changing to showcase the latest acquisition.

Family heirlooms play an important part in the design scheme. Many of the sewing tools and notions were used by several generations of ancestors. Along with photographs of these women and a few remnants of their work, they invoke gratitude for inherited skills and provide encouragement at difficult times.

A modern sewing machine is flanked by antiques that provide practical storage space, several kinds of inspiration, or simply add a note of whimsy. At its left is a spool cabinet that first held great-grandmother's sewing supplies, then those of the three succeeding generations. Above it, on the left, a World War I era ad for fabric dye promises this year's fashions from last year's clothes with just an inexpensive color change.

Above the machine, the drawer from an old type case is perfect for keeping spools of thread in view and for displaying tiny treasures. The corkboard below it holds pattern instructions, fabric swatches to ponder, design sketches to consider, and photos to enjoy.

The office chair—a flea market bargain—is built to reduce fatigue. A bright new cover hides all traces of its corporate character.

7

Sewing Room Inspiration

The ultimate sewing accessory is of course the space where you work. No matter whether it is just a corner of the family room or a full-scale studio, it is a better place when a little of your creative time is put toward making it all your own, arranged to suit your needs and decorated to please you.

On these pages are photos of two exceptional sewing rooms to inspire your own ideas. They are as different as two rooms can be, yet each is designed to work perfectly for its occupant, providing exactly the atmosphere to keep her creative spirits high.

ALONG the top of the type drawer are antique photos, buttons, and buckles. The handkerchief is an heirloom that the designer carried at her wedding. The silver thimbles down the right side were used by five great-aunts.

WHEN Great-grandfather installed a bathroom in the early 1880's, this ornate medicine cabinet began its service. Today it houses an assortment of trims and sewing gear in fine style.

AT the window, mannequin arms serve as a most distinctive swag holder. The swag itself might be the latest irresistible fabric purchase, or a great find from an estate sale.

The ironing board is set low for quick pressing from a seated position. The old iron is in perfect working order; it is much heavier than the modern counterparts and more effective at bonding fusibles and taming difficult-to-press fabrics.

The dress form sports a pincushion top to keep pins handy for fittings. Above it, a schoolroom coat rack keeps master patterns in order.

A **SAMPLING** of the room's button collection includes some heirlooms, some antique shop finds, and a few recent additions.

Fine pearl buttons deserve to be salvaged from worn garments, and to be on display until they are attached to new ones.

A Custom-Built Room for Maximum Efficiency

designer:
Joyce Baldwin

WITH clean lines, soft color, and not a bit of wasted space, this superbly planned room can't help but inspire a sewer's best efforts. The room's designer took a year just to fine-tune the plans and ideas she had accumulated over a lifetime of sewing.

This room, like the preceding one, is quite small, yet every inch of space is put to good use. The result is a completely efficient and thoroughly comfortable place to work.

The designer offers a few good suggestions to other sewers who may be contemplating an equally extensive design project:

- Work with a good professional cabinet-maker. A knowledgeable professional will be aware of all kinds of specialized materials and hardware that can work well with your design.

- List what you have to store—fabric, threads, all the tools, pressing equipment, rulers, shears. For those materials that tend to accumulate, such as fabric, patterns, books, trims, and thread, allow space for future acquisitions.

- Think about future equipment purchases, too. Do you plan to buy a serger? Iron press? New sewing machine? Build in some flexibility.

- Don't forget lighting needs. In addition to the sewing area itself, plan for lighting at the cutting table and ironing board. Be sure the existing wiring can accommodate any scheduled additions.

A GENEROUSLY sized work counter accommodates the sewing machine and serger. Above, a corkboard displays instructions for the current project and inspiration for future ones. Decorative baskets on the upper shelves maintain order among the less frequently used gadgets and supplies. Drawers on either side of the knee space hold machine accessories and often-used tools and supplies.

This designer, too, appreciates the value of a good chair—and also has chosen to re-cover its industrial upholstery.

BELOW the work counter, specially designed drawers hold spools of thread of every conceivable size and shape.

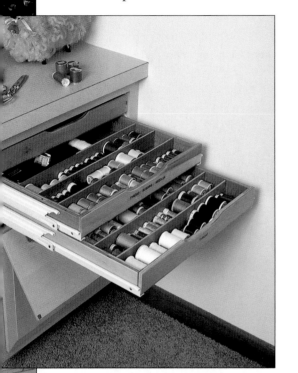

THE wall adjacent to the sewing area is entirely taken up by a multi-purpose cabinet. With all doors closed, only the spacious bookshelves are visible.

The upper left section provides dust-free storage for an extensive fabric collection. Transparent boxes exactly fit the shelves. Below the bookshelves are pattern storage drawers and enclosed shelves to hold miscellaneous supplies. The right section of the cabinet houses a fold-down ironing board with its own spotlight above. The storage space below is sized just for videos.

$A^\mathbf{T}$ the end is a small closet containing additional shelves for books and pressing equipment, along with hanging space for garments in progress. There is a full-length mirror inside of the door. Reflected in the mirror is the wall opposite, with a computer desk—fast becoming a sewing room necessity.

$T^{\mathbf{HE}}$ remarkable cutting table, with drop leaves extended, nearly fills the room. It can accommodate a two-yard length of fabric, and provides additional storage space as well. The space below holds drafting supplies and cutting equipment as well as an additional drawer on each side for patterns.

WE ARE MOST GRATEFUL TO THE DESIGNERS
who conjured up and created the models for the projects shown on the preceding pages. Most of them are professional sewers, and many of their designs were developed to fulfill their own sewing room requirements.

The Designers

A very special thanks to Pat Scheible and Joyce Baldwin who kindly allowed us to photograph their extraordinary sewing rooms.

Joyce Baldwin has designed clothing throughout her life, and enjoys other forms of needle art just as much. She teaches courses in textiles and apparel at Western Carolina University.

Beth Hill specializes in superbly crafted bears that find their way to homes around the country. Experimentation with embroidery and clothing designs occupies her "free" time.

Lori Kerr designs fabric jewelry and textile art pieces, specializing in applique. She enjoys, above all, sharing her skills through classes and workshops.

Suzanne Koppi has sewn professionally for many years, pursuing every sewing angle. She has recently retired from a special education career and plans to devote more time to fabric.

Dale Liles is a professional felt-maker. In addition to making one-of-a-kind wearables, she spends a good part of her year traveling around the globe to teach felt-making workshops.

Elizabeth Searle is a dressmaker by profession. After a long day in her workroom she relaxes with sewing machine play!

Marion Mulford studied haute couture in Europe. She is a custom dressmaker, and produces garments for the major pattern companies' catalogs.

Mary Parker finds sewing a rewarding form of relaxation. She teaches classes, particularly in her own machine Sashiko technique, and experiments with every new sewing technique she discovers.

Nell Paulk experiments with just about all of the needle arts, applying her design talents to fabrics and yarns of every description.

Judith Robertson actually sews up most of the fabric she acquires, a noteworthy accomplishment. Most of her creative efforts are put toward clothing design and embellishment.

Laura Rohde sews professionally and for fun as well. She works primarily with weavers, designing and producing garments from handwoven fabrics.

Pat Scheible, a decorative painter by trade, designs and creates with fiber, paint, and most any other materials that strike her fancy.

Terry Taylor is an artist whose work takes many forms and invariably includes some stitching and a bit of fabric.

Dee Dee Triplett considers doll-making her primary focus, and teaches her craft at workshops around the country. She always enjoys the challenge of creating useful articles—as long as they have some visual appeal.

Index